The Next Messiah

You!

The Next Messiah

You!

by

Michael J. David

Book 1

One Spirit Press
Portland, Oregon

One Spirit Press,
onespiritpress@gmail.com
www.onespiritpress.com

Portland, Oregon

Dedication

To all those who would seek to know and understand Truth.

And to my family, Guides and those who helped me along the path.

Content

Each Warrior wants to leave the mark of his will, his signature, on important acts he touches. This is not the voice of ego but of the human spirit, rising up and declaring that it has something to contribute to the solution of the hardest problems, no matter how vexing!

Pat Riley

Nor shall derision prove powerful against those who listen to humanity or those who follow in the footsteps of divinity, for they shall live forever. Forever.

Khalil Gibran

Anytime there is a struggle between doing what is actually right and doing what seems right, then your ego is interfering with your decision.

Darren L. Johnson

God-Consciousness and Ego

These are the most powerful forces in our world today!

The ego mind has destroyed our world in a short time when compared to the God-Consciousness, which existed before humankind came to earth. Soon there will be a reckoning between the two forces that will end in a new consciousness descending over the earth that will nurture all life as we know it. It is a time of choosing between wrong and right, dark and light, Ego and God-Consciousness.

Illusion and Reality

Trying to make ends meet we focus on the *rat race*. If you're lucky to know all the right people and you have a great product, you might make it to the top 1% of all that are deemed fiscally successful.

When you see success as connected to material wealth you are living a deep part of illusion! Ego is a state of mind that distorts the nature of reality (spirit) and keeps us locked into a kind of prison of illusion. We create an identity that is false, an identity based on who we think we are because of our parents, where we were born and when. Getting past the ego and the illusions is one of the hardest lessons of our time. Our entire world has been formed to live in nothing but ego mind. We have been raised to fear, live, and die as an ego identity.

Illusion has taught us to fear other people; it causes war, famine, and death. It has given us poor attitudes toward others, the need to control people and situations. This ego reigns within government and life.

The illusion is just that! Illusion! All these things that we have become are the same things we dread becoming every day. In spite of our dread, the illusion prevails in the world.

My parents were typical of people living the hippie days in the late sixties. My father was breaking free from his military training while my mother was attending nursing school. They were evolving to a new level of consciousness, with a family and bills to pay. And all the time they were following the rules of ego.

They needed a bigger home for two children with a big back yard and with this came the bills and eventually a large car or station wagon. And then with the home came the military Sunday BBQ's and girl's night and eventually a maid. And all the time they had to earn more money to pay for the additional life style. It is a tumbling effect in life. When people hit a major roadblock such as divorce, well, this is when reality, God-Consciousness, sets in.

Reality pulls us back toward our original life plan, the actual reason we venture here in the first place. Otherwise, why come to the one place where everyone is out to get you! Or so it seems. Think about it; everything you do; everywhere you go; all the people you don't meet. Why? Have you ever been driving down a road and noticed that there are hundreds of cars around you and if you're lucky one person might look at you with a smile on their face? Why is that? Have you ever considered that you, too, never look or smile or even wave at another? All of this is based on ego mind, the fear factor of life. I don't want to look at him or her for fear they may chase me down and kill me! I'm afraid of what they may do! I'm tired! They're tired! Why should I look at them, I don't know them! I don't care!

All of this brings into our lives more fear, hatred, and destruction. This alone empowers the ego!

Reality is what we don't see all that often. Such as the love, the kind individual that helps another to the other side of the road, someone who gives you money for no other reason than you needed it right then. As well as the people who go out of their way to assist the elderly or the children without being paid.

A company that gives without requiring anything in return is now working in reality. The Mother that gives natural birth to her baby is now working in reality. The person that gives an organ to another that is in need of it is now working in reality.

Reality is a form of understanding about giving and receiving without the energy exchange of money! It is the form of love that doesn't fear anything or anyone. It is you!

What Does It Mean?

Ego-Principle is the illusion of our entire world today. It is the reflection of destruction even in a natural setting. To explain; If the natural path of nature is shifted because of humankind's greed, by something such as an oil spill, it causes a shift in nature's evolution. We are linked with nature. We know this; we live it every day. When something happens that is destructive to our way of life then we say God did this to us or it was a natural disaster, when all along we were the ones to create, empower, and destroy. We are the trigger. Let me explain. We are the trigger causing global warming, removing the natural energies of the earth, creating smog, and by cutting down the ancient trees that clean our world and give us fresh air. We are the trigger and yet we are not doing anything about it, or at least nothing that stops the trigger. So, naturally, we are seeing severe weather storms, higher water in the lower areas of land, increased volcanic activity, and all the time most say, "Well, it is a natural disaster." Or is it?

Mother Nature is a form of energy we call Earth. No one disputes this until we introduce God-Consciousness reality and then it suddenly becomes a question of religion instead of Reality!

The Reality is that the Earth (Mother Nature) is trying to change in order to meet the demands of her inhabitants. However, she can only change so fast and therefore she is much more violent than if we slowed our consumption down significantly.

The Earth wasn't formed in two hundred years and yet, in this same amount of time we managed to burn down forests and remove the trees for paper and fuel. We managed to take the oil from the Earth to burn it as fossil fuel.

Yes, it is here for our use. However, the greed of ego has taken advantage of this natural resource and now God-Consciousness reality is setting in to resolve the matter.

Where Do We Go From Here

Life evolves, no matter if our generation is willing or not! We now can make a significant difference with all generations. We need to take the initiative and say enough is enough. Ego is no longer the ruling party in our lives! We choose to live conscious reality.

When a mass of people believe one way to be true and their truth doesn't improve life but, in fact, makes it worse, there needs to be a major change and/or event take place in order to shake the people awake again. This shake down change is called 2012.

This is the very change that we need to make a go of a new life with our abilities. It is the shift of consciousness that will start the healing process of the earth and the people as well as the other inhabitants upon it.

We go where we are not comfortable going, we go and say hello to our neighbor, we smile at a stranger, and we wave a friendly gesture to anyone. We stop using others to better ourselves. We stop being selfish and we focus on selflessness!

We can change from what we know of disaster and destruction in ego to healing, peacefulness, compassion, caring, and love for all of the Earth and her inhabitants. Now that doesn't sound so bad, does it!

Here's the catch: Ego has ruled the earth for thousands of years. Even when Jesus and the others, now Ascended Masters, came and tried to warn us of our ego actions and help us to see the healing and love that is available, we still continued to allow ego to rule. While we think we are right within the ego, it is still illusion and illusion will not survive in the new world past 2012. Yet, as we have learned, all things can change on a dime. People don't generally accept change that fast and therefore we fight any change forced upon us. This revealed within all of the movies and other paraphernalia that indicate severe and tragic losses.

Once people change and accept a new healthy way of thinking and under-standing, then our consciousness will evolve and we will better understand the nature of reality and absolute love.

This is the reality that is set forth for our very near future!

Applying this Knowledge Successfully

The belief comes first. The belief that healing is possible from all of the ail-ments we suffer such as dis-ease, dis-orders, loss of life, depressions, and any other type of life changing event.

Here is how it works: You seek out a professional and I'm not talking about someone that is crazy with ambitions, but has no knowledge of the work that is necessary for this type of change. You are fighting against thousands of years of life paths and evolution in order to right yourself.

Look at this from another point of view. Think about a boat, if it is sitting upright in the water then the boat is level and in a healthy state. If the boat starts to take on water the boat will start to list to one side. Now the boat is either listing right or left and is no longer in good standing. The boat now has a serious problem and unless something happens to remove the weight imbalance the boat will either roll completely over and sink or just simply sink beneath the waterline to its death on the ocean floor. We are aboard the illusion (ego-principle) of life and the weight of the illusionary knowledge is just about to roll us over and sink us. We can bail ourselves out by changing our train of thought from the illusion to reality by listening and working on skill level development with other reality (God Consciousness) profession-als that do nothing but communicate the positive will of all.

These professionals are all over the world. Some live right next to you. You may even know several of us. These professionals work in many fields such as healing, hypnosis, holistic health care, natural foods and more. We are focused now on how to stay healthy and to clean up our eating habits and to focus on cleaning up our own attitudes. This is called Skill Level Develop-ment and in order for all of us to recover from our illusionary lives we must learn Skill Level Development. No, it doesn't mean you have to switch the type of work you do or the type of person you wish to date, either. It does mean that you do need to focus yourself on developing what will feel like new skills in communications. However, you will simply be remembering skills that you have already developed in different life paths of your souls past lives.

Once you complete the many different Skill Levels of conscious awakening you will find that you will lose weight easier, look younger, feel lighter, live healthier, and become much happier. You will find that you want to live a longer life. You will work less and smarter and you will love deeper and longer than you ever thought you could. All because you gave yourself a chance to change from ego to a conscious reality!

As our new conscious shift changes and completes its cycle you will find that the world will shift from night to day. Think of it like this; have you ever seen a dark street with only one light on it? Well, think of all of the professional instructors as the light and the rest of the darkness is everyone that wishes to dilute themselves in Ego. What happens when the light goes out? Chaos ensues. However, if the light is joined by many other lights, of various vibrations and intensities. you will have a football field of light and so on. All those in the dark will draw to the light and thus you will have balance.
In the world today, we have so many that live in the dark-night (Ego-Principle illusion) and they are searching for the light-day (God-Consciousness Reality). 2012 gives us the chance to open the doors to Reality so that everyone can now see and live in the daylight.

NOTES

How people treat you is their karma; how you react is yours.

Wayne Dyer

Bridging the Laws of Karma

Humanity is neither illusion nor reality. It does represent what people believe they are. Our beliefs place us into a box. Must of us are terrified of our true-selves.

Humanity is nothing more than the individuation of spirit, formed into masses of people formed together as one. God Consciousness is all there is. Your soul does not exist in a box. And the soul defies a simple description. Your soul is the whole of your existence speaking to you every day.

Everywhere there is negativity which creates fear, war, anguish, sadness, depression, sickness, dis-ease, dis-order and eventually chaos. This is a kind of negative Karma, which is wide spread through society.

The balance of Karma must happen. In the infinite there is only balance. In the Earthly world you have lived, you have so much negativity and you have grown with the understanding that this is the "norm" and you have forgotten your balance your being.

As you have grown with the concepts of negative thought you will now grow with positive thoughts. The ego of humanity does not like change. As a species we do not take lightly to change. Even thinking of this change is a very positive one. It is best explained in this term; If you where to place a frog in cold water, what would the frog do? The frog would remain in the water! Now, turn up the volume of heat slowly at first and what does the frog do now? They remain in the water and eventually the frog will die from the heat. Why you say? The slow raising of the temp does not alert the frog it must change. Humanity is similar, it gets use to the negative thought over time not recognizing that it is destroying because over time one doesn't see the changes that are needed to happen in order for humanity not to overheat it's self.

As human beings we have turned up the heat (negativity) slowly over thousands of years. And now we are at the critical point of passing or are we at the point of change? Yes, change, that can make us see the light so suddenly that we don't boil to death.

Humanity doesn't want to understand Karma. Humankind is simply willing to judge others Karma. Karma is now playing out for all of humanity. Only when as a species we start seeing the necessity of understanding the ego will we begin to see the positive side of ego. We learn through mistakes. By acknowledging and accepting responsibility we become like a stone dropped in a pool, sending out our new awareness to all of humanity.

How the Laws of Karma Effect You

As life has evolved on this planet so has Karma. As we struggle for a new understanding of our life so does the planet struggle to find the sacred balance of life that unfolds.

Karma affects change in all of us. All the time as energy continues to move through and around each and every one of us. You see it every day of your life while in this earthly vessel. Karma is all around you and it is you.

Karma is sometimes referred to;

- Well, they had that one coming to them!

- It must have been karma!

- Or even sometimes people will say that's good karma.

See, it is all around you. For example; Let's say you wound up in a car accident and you truly where not the one at fault, how do you interpret it? Do you say well that was Karma? Where does your mind take you during such an undertaking in your life?

Most people will jump to conclusion using black and white ego judgment..

Your true answer should be yes, it was Karma. And they are the ones now suffering for the accident. However, so are you! Does this mean that you too are suffering from negative Karma? Yes and no. First, the yes part, you have chosen to live the little bit of karma that the accident did to you and this will create balance for you in your life. Second, the No part, your right to free will allowed you to make a decision to balance your Karma. In this manner, you have freely allowed Karma to balance your life. If you respond to the accident in a negative ego driven thought process you give negative energy to your current situation. This then creates another in balance in the Laws of Karma.

The effects of Karma are very simply explained; if you do something negative to another then something negative will happen to you! If you do something positive to another then something positive will happen to you. You are one with all existence, and all the answers to life are within you. Activate positive energy and live a positive life!

Balance the Final Frontier

If we have a war then the balance will be peace. Or is it? If we fall then we rise, right? If we experience yin than we will feel yang! If we have bad weather then we have good weather. Do you see the point?

You're in a state of balance right now. You may have lived a life full of negativity for many years, and now you are starting to live a life full of positivity. This is balance.

The final frontier of balance is the consciousness shift of negative energies to positive energies. It is that simple, and yet complex!

The simple part is the difference between negative and positive energy. The complex part is very difficult to get the humanity to change from a negative way of life to a positive living and a new healthier way of life.

Have you ever noticed how the masses follow each other blindly? Why is that? Why would we want to follow a group of people without discussion to how that will affect us? Will we be lost in the group or is this a benefit to our growth. To accept without thought and question is to be ego driven by the collective unconscious.

When we lose our vision of why we came here in the first place we lose our way and suddenly we feel alone. This is when fear sets in and we don't think about how it will affect us so much as to how we can simply fit in again.

Fear monger leadership happens when we allow leaders to persuade us we are without power and frighten us about a basic need of some sort. We never choose to take back our own power because we are afraid of judgment. We are afraid that we will be thrown away with the rest of those people that have tried before us such as Jesus and other ascended masters and then negativity will prevail. However, if we apply positive energy to any situation over time we will warm the waters of humanity to a positive nature.

Balance is simply returning negative energy to positive.

Never Say Never

When we fight with what will be we miss what can be! Our ego has been fighting against the positive energies that will heal us. You are the holder of your power and you don't even realize it. Those of you who have learned that you hold your own torch of life are now terrified of the abundance of it. And those of you who have tried to use it against others are now seeing the faults of your own work.

STOP for a moment stand back from yourself, and study what has become and study what you can do to change it in a positive manner.

Those who say "never", well then be lost to yourself in the illusion known has ego!

Those of you who say "maybe" will then have a chance to change and grow with the world as you delve into the reality known as God Consciousness. This is a positive forum which will allow you to grow with The Laws of Karma and yet allow you to live a positive and healthy life style.

We say, "Never say Never". Otherwise you condemn yourselves to a life of misery! Do you really want to continue this life seeing only negativity? Or would you like a fresh chance at living a life full of prosperity and love. Yes you can, and yes you will.

Remember to take your power back. Remember to live within every moment and remember to be positive about everything you do. You will find that you will attract positive energy into your life.

Remember if you decide to say "Never" you may in fact cause this statement to effect your entire souls journey, not just this lifetime! So focus on what you really want and remember to ask for it in the most positive thought and words.

NOTES

I believe you make your day. You make your life. So much of it is all perception, and this is the form that I built for myself. I have to accept it and work within those compounds, and it's up to me.

Brad Pitt

Perception

What Does It Really Mean?

We perceive through our consciousness as well as the collective unconscious of humanity. Only through self-observation can we know if we are using our ego to define what the senses are reporting or if we are getting a true input from God Consciousness.

Perception is colored, changed, and focused through our beliefs, prejudices, and memories in the unconscious mind. No one can see or perceive another's sight. Our beginning perceptions are mostly based on surface stimuli that trigger beliefs and working paradigms in the unconscious mind.

Even the most gifted psychic or intuitive must filter through their unconscious mind. They quickly learn to know what resides in the unconscious mind so they can understand the information they are receiving. Only by using self observation can an intuitive be clear as to what is coming from the God Consciousness we all carry.

It is important to remember our views of perception must be defined through the perception of God Consciousness and not through our ego centered self that uses beliefs and prejudices to draw conclusions. Simply put, if you have always perceived through Ego Principle the illusion, well then you must now flip the thought to God Consciousness reality.

Let's examine this from another point of view. Let's say you are dyslexic and you see the world in reverse and you are taught through ego that the world you're viewing is backwards yet you feel wrong about changing it. Which is true? Isn't it possible that the dyslexic may have had the energy right the first time!

See we are gifted with many people that perceive the world for what it truly is in Reality and yet we tell the ADD person that they're wrong, why? Isn't it possible we have it perceived in a prejudice manner? What defines the norm to perceive for the rest of the people?

In today's world, we perceive violence that comes from those suppressed or inflated in society. Yes, I said inflated!

There have been many that have inflated salaries or personalities and ego that are the size of the moon and they are perceived to be violent. Maybe not with a gun., but they control the masses with money! I have it and you don't. Then we fall into the age-old adage of trying to get the money; and yet the answer to the situation is too simple. Do without the money and then their power is no longer! Your perception of the situation changes and so does those who have control in the first place.

Yes, yes, yes, I realize that the world is perceived around money, but what is money? Money is ink on a piece of bark! How did we get the bark? We harvest it. So if you harvest bark and created ink is it not so hard to harvest food and sell it at a market or exchange it for whatever is needed?

See it is all in our perception of how we wish to live life. Whether it is in ego or reality, it is your choice, it is your perception, and it is you're reality to live!

The water glass is half full or half empty

We are so consumed with personal perception it isn't even funny and yet like a dyslexic we are so confused about which way is up or down or front or back. We have lost our way. There are many people around trying to help us find our way. Not just people, but your spirit guides are working overtime to help you find yourself.

The water glass is half anything; does it really matter whether it is full or empty? Yes, it does. Why, if you perceive your emotions being half full then you are allowing positive energies to fill your glass. If you perceive your emotions to be full then you are not allowing yourself to receive anything. It is a difficult equation when it is broken down. Simply put, it is better to have your emotions purged from time to time so that you can receive positive energies to replace any negative energy.

Just as we view the glass is only half full or half empty, there are those in the world today who perceive optimism or pessimism this way. Life is about our perception. We are perceiving everywhere and in everything we do from the time we wake till we fall asleep. Even when we sleep or minds are still processing we call it sub-consciousness. We are perceiving 24 hours a day 7 days a week.

The question remains how do you perceive your life: half full or half empty?

The end of days

I can't tell you how many times I have heard that 2012 means we are at the end of days! It is getting really annoying that so many people don't realize it isn't the end of the world as we know it! It is a shift in the world consciousness as we know it from ego to a new reality.

This simplicity is lost as tabloids, newspapers, authors and movie productions go right for the negative in everything. We seem to respond quickly to the negative. How much will it take for us to finally say, "Stop being so negative" really! Would you allow your child to be this negative? Do you want your spouse to be this negative?

Life isn't negative when your baby is born! Life isn't negative when you share your first kiss, love and union with another. We have so much to share that is positive that we need to balance out energies with a new consciousness shift.

The shift of 2012 has much to offer us. It will give us the tools through the professionals that heeded the warnings early. This shift began in 1987! Those professionals are all around you, everywhere. You have to be smart enough to look for them or simple enough to open your eyes and see them next to you!

If you follow 2012 through ego you will suffer intensely. If you cause yourself to suffer it is free will, your choice. You have the right to choose what you do. You always have this right and it is up to you to choose how you will perceive

Our New Beginning

As our world shifts from negative to positive energy reality, many will suffer. Many people may not shift so easily and that saddens me greatly. It is your choice to choose to shift you're perception. Be forwarned that if you choose to follow the ego principle your life will suffer greatly. The God Consciousness reality is already underway and it will cause those whom choose not to follow great pain.

If you choose to follow the consciousness shift to reality you will learn quickly how to apply you're new found abilities to your day-to-day intuitive lives. Your life becomes much happier as you start to live your true-life plan, which you decide before being born on this planet.

Remember you have a new beginning being offered to you right now. As the world changes and gears up for this new eye opening experience of positive energies, you have the right to enjoy it too.

Now if you are really comfortable and financially stable you may feel compelled to help a lot more people, who all need a break with assistance. This is a positive reaction with reality.

If you are a billionaire and you have several millions to assist others to learn about their intuitive awareness this will open up positive energies around you. All of these methods are not just based on money. The same can be applied by love, compassion, generosity, food, and so much more.

For thousands of years we survived without technology, as we know it today. We survived without transportation as we know it today and frankly we can again if we have too. So, think about this new beginning, think of how you would like it to affect your lives and then focus that thought on a positive outcome, you may surprise yourself. Our lives are short lived in this space, time, and plane so let's make the best of it as we are here to learn.

Life 2013

Do you know how you perceive our world today? We tend to perceive it with a shade of grey over everything and that grey is getting darker with every day.   After we shift our consciousness through 2012 and we realign our thoughts and positive outcomes this thick grey will lift and suddenly you will see life as it really is.

Imagine looking at a plant or flower and seeing it shaded with grey then lift the grey off and you see the sun hit the flower and it is so bright and absolutely the most beautiful thing you have ever seen. This is, as the world really is, and you are just now opening up to it. Just as you allowed yourself to see the flower as it really is.

Allow 2013 to be your light at the end of your tunnel. Allow it to give you a sense of direction and a goal to achieve. You won't be disappointed by your own actions and you will be the ones that made it all happen.

NOTES

A Prayer of Spiritual Prosperity

Thank You, Father, for your kind and generous spirit within me. Your unlimited abundance prospers and blesses my life.

Your infinite Spirit is my one source of abundance. I put my faith in You, God, knowing that You will guide and direct me in receiving all that my heart desires.

Thank You, God, for your unending wisdom and inspiration. You fill my mind with prosperous visions and ideas. Thank you for your all-knowing presence that helps me to receive the physical and spiritual prosperity that you would will for me. My life is rich and abundant in every way.

You are my one true source, dear God, and in your presence every need is met, every desire is answered. I am grateful for your overflowing love that blesses me and everyone in my life.

God, Your blessings fill my heart and mind and attract to me all good things. Through your infinite essence, I know I am always taken care of and have everything that I truly want and need.

The Voice of Love Website

Spiritual Prosperity

What is spiritual prosperity?

Now that's a good question, Webster's Dictionary defines it like this:

The condition of being successful or thriving, especially economic wellbeing.

A successful, flourishing, or thriving condition, especially in financial respects; good fortune

Prosperities; prosperous circumstances

When we follow spirit through God Consciousness Reality the redefinitions are as follows:

1. Spiritual Prosperity is the state of God Consciousness that flourishes within each of our souls.

2. Spiritual Prosperity encompasses the wealth of unconditional love for a balance within God Consciousness.

3. The basics of Spiritual Prosperity become the wealth of understanding within your true intuition.

Spiritual Prosperity isn't about your finances, it is about the unconditional love that we feel with our children, with our pets, with our plants, with bodies of water or just about anything that you can sit in peace with and share this unconditional love.

Think about it like this for a moment. Imagine you're with your grandparents and your grandmother shares some gardening tips with you. How do you consider this?   Another way to look at this is; imagine you're with your grandfather and you are fishing together. How do you consider this?

In both circumstances, this would be unconditional love being shared with you in both situations. This is spiritual prosperity!

Let us examine from another point of view. Let's say for a moment that you are spiritually aware of your spirit guides and you are able to communicate with them. Have you ever felt unsafe with them around? Or have you always felt peace with them? This again would be spiritual prosperity.

This works in all environments at all times as we are one energy.   So the next time your outside and the sun is shining brightly in the sky think about the blade of grass beneath your feet and the rose blooming in full color and the soft clouds over head. These are all spiritual prosperities in one form or another.

How can Spiritual Prosperity help me Become Prosperous?

By changing your thinking patterns, how you think and your emotional direction.

Spiritual Prosperity isn't just going to church and paying your five dollars every Sunday. It is much more than just sitting in church and listening to the Pastor speak. It is deeper than going to bible studies and speaking the words of the bible.

When we speak of Spiritual Prosperity we are talking about the very essence of our lives, our bodies, and our souls. It is the way in which we absorb thoughts and how we share these thoughts with others.

In war, people are not given a choice to suffer through the ego of others but are made to suffer through the ego of others thoughts. How ever we suffer through physical pain for the ego prosperity of others, it is then that we, those whom have suffered this physical pain, show our best in spiritual prosperity through unconditional love for others in the same situation. We reach out of our comfort zone to help out as much as possible each situation. It is in our hour of need that spiritual prosperity shows its true colors in us all.

In times of peace, spiritual prosperity is strong as we prosper with education and the many millions of foundations that help the needy and the many different companies that help those who don't have their homes anymore or those that need newer homes to live in. It is the lost pet that seeks shelter or the dog next door that needs water. It is the thought of helping anything or everything around you.

Along my journey I have found spiritual prosperity in the strangest of places. One day I was working as a truck driver and I saw a hawk on top of a seagull and I started to feel (unconditional love) for the seagull so I called in thought The Father and asked for love and light to save this seagull. Within a minute, the hawk flew away and the seagull got up and shook its wings. Then it looked at me just as astonished as I looked at it, then it flew away. It was the most beautiful thing I had ever experienced in my life! The spiritual prosperity was strong and it felt really good afterwards. A shift in my consciousness allowed me to see past myself long enough to recognize another for assistance.

Spiritual Prosperity is good for everything you do. You can apply it to any situation and the situation will turn out wonderful for you. And if it doesn't, then look at your true intentions.

Practice with it on a couple of situations. Remember we human beings are creatures of habit and the more times we practice the better we become at our tasks. Always keep an open mind and an open heart for the best results.

Religion of Dogma

For thousands of years people have followed all sorts of religious beliefs. Almost always those who found spiritual prosperity found it outside of the church dogma. They found it through meditation, prayer and epiphanies. We are taught we are to follow the religion of dogma and if we don't the end is always the same. We will die in sin.

There is nothing such as sin. Sin is an old archers term that meant to miss the mark. Sin is nothing more than a misunderstanding of spiritual law, the Truth. When you choose to follow unfounded rules of any one religious dogma rather than understanding your true identity as truth, spirit, you live outside of the spiritual. This in turns causes you to fear. The devil and sin are nothing more than this fear. Fear mongering has been a kind of leadership for thousands of years. When a mass of individuals are afraid, they will follow the person or idea that seems to relieve them or save them from the fearful predictions. Many religions have created fear to keep aspirants loyal. Spiritual understanding and law dispel the idea that fear is needed or exists. When a person is spiritually mature, they grasp the idea that all life is connected. Your life is filled with unconditional love. Straight thinking allows leaders to produce a whole new existence for aspirants. Fear doesn't enter into the equation.

With spiritual prosperity you choose what you believe and you choose what you want to love or not. You are defined by your relationship with Truth/God/Consciousness, not by a physical body, or fear of hell, or sin.

Spirituality in Humanity

We, as intelligent beings (the soul), manifest as the appearance of matter (the body). We have the ability to transcend, which means we have chosen to transcend from our original homes. We choose to come here and live and work with routines and grow with learning lessons. We chose our life paths and all of the lessons that we can learn while here in these physical bodies.

Although we remember either very little of our prior spiritual life, or we remember nothing and we develop in this space, time, and plane to learn of our Spiritual Prosperity.

Once we have developed enough for this spiritual path we then start to learn of who we really are. A classic saying by Eckhart Tolle is "What is, is". This would be the best rendition in our earthly vocabulary in a very basic way of explaining life and all its complexities!

Some say you can't fight "truth", and they are right. I have seen many try and yet fail every time because "what is, is", is the truth! You are a spiritual being. You are a spiritual being having a human experience. It appears this experience helps us understand our relation to the creator source/Truth/God/Consciousness.

 Now this doesn't mean you are a "religious fanatic". It does mean, however, that you are much more than just a thing. You are a being of light energy and intelligence beyond imagination. This much is true and you are here to learn through millions of learning lessons to perfect your soul's life in this space, time, and plane by your choice.

Yes, you made the choice to develop on this level of existence. And you, by just reading this far, have learned that you have the ability to change your perspective on all thoughts in this life. See it is a matter of choices, your choices.

A Time Without Unconditional Love

We have been lead to believe that the days of the world of unconditional love are coming to an end. Mankind in its weakest of forms is taught to fear and with this fear the end of the world is here.

Now look at this from another point of view. Think of or imagine the world as we currently know it without unconditional love, even in the smallest of situations. Wouldn't this mean kayos? You wouldn't be able to make love because you don't have unconditional love for another. You wouldn't have friendships and you wouldn't have parties and you wouldn't share stories and so on.

See unconditional love is all around you and so spiritual prosperity is all around you. If you, through fear, remove these things or even control them then suddenly you are just a piece of machine working for the greed of man every day and night. Life is meant to be lived, which means we are to live in love and light, not in the dark and dreary. It is only man that has changed life by the choices of fear and greed.

We have the unprecedented opportunity to live in light and love and to show others they can also live in light and love. This is what God is all about sharing a very unique experience in the love and light of God. The sooner we realize greed and fear are no longer profitable, the negative energies will fall away and true unconditional love will emerge and show its absolute beautiful face once again.

The Differences Between Illusion and Reality

What is the difference between illusion and reality? Through self-observation, we can learn to see our ego at work. We can see it try to manipulate and distort our identity. Illusion is seeing the oasis and believing it to be real. When we see our physical world and think it solid and immovable we are witnessing ego at work. Truth is the reality. Truth is that which is so, that which is not truth is not so, is nothing, there for truth is all there is, this is the reality of life, the nature of reality, God/Truth/Consciousness is all there is. By understanding that our senses see and experience life as starting and stopping, we begin to see how we buy into the illusion. True spirituality sees the reality of life is the existential connections we make. We do not end at our fingertips nor do we begin. Reality is ever evenly present without beginning or end.

DE'JA'VU

I have heard so many people say they have experienced De'Ja'Vu and yet they seem to think it really strange that they would have this ability. What fascinates me the most is when they say I have been here before, but that is impossible! Why is that so impossible to have been here before? Well many don't believe in reincarnation and so there is no way they would believe that they came through this very same life once before. In fact they may have traveled this time more than once. Sometimes it takes us a couple of tries to compete the learning task at hand.

We choose our life paths, but if we take ourselves out too early or someone takes our life then we return to complete it. It is that simple. So it is entirely possible that one may have been here more than one time. Each time you come back the circumstances will have changed because you will have achieved a certain level in each of your lessons that you first choose to study.

The landscape may be the same and this is what you recognize. Don't be discouraged if you come back, you get a second or third chance to finish that life experience.

I used to worry over returning a couple of times to this life, but I soon settled down about it as I realized that God wasn't disappointed in me. I believed, by way of fear, that if I had returned then I had done something really bad. But now I realize that isn't the case and I'm pleased as punch to know that we have a God that is ever merciful.

I had an interesting experience once as I was walking into a McDonalds to enjoy some French fries with my best friend. As we walked through the entry door I felt like I bumped into someone and they sounded like two women. It was really interesting. My best friend was like, "Wow! Are you ok?" I said, "Yes. I think I just ran into two women." She said, "Are you sure?" I said, "Yes. I think they are just asking themselves the same thing."

See, we are so close to the next dimension that sometimes you can feel others around you. This isn't crazy talk, but reality!

Was That a Coincidence?

Have you thought about a friend you haven't seen in sometime? You will sit there and think about this person for a little bit of time and then you go on about your day, thinking from time to time about this wonderful friend and all the good and bad times you shared with each other. And then you get to your phone and see that the very person you where thinking off has indeed called you. Is that Coincidence?

We are all connected. The Chinese often joke about the ability to know before a telephone rings. The connection is the universal unconscious mind. There are no coincidences or accidents. We are always in the right place at the right time according to our state of awareness. In the realm of spiritual law all is perfect according to God/Truth.

The universe is one great symphony and each of us play an instrument in this orchestra. Our sense of reality is the notes we play out. Our consciousness brings us to the many different songs we all play in the symphony of life. We are always at the right place at the right time and there are no accidents or coincidences.

What ever is in our consciousness we attract. What we know, we attract to us. What we understand, we attract to us. To fear God is to know God. Originally, the word fear meant to know. We can attract what we love or fear. We experience and attract that which abides in our consciousness. Only through self-observation and understanding our unconscious mind can we begin to understand why some of the things happen in our life. You don't have to do anything to use the law of attraction. It happens all the time. What we know or understand we attract to us.

When we speak of choosing we are not speaking of choosing a flavor of ice cream. The choices we make are not always conscious. Most choices come from our unconscious mind and we are not aware that we are making them. We don't wish to be ill, or choose to be ill. Deep in our subconscious mind we make choices that produce illness. Only by understanding what resides in the subconscious mind can we understand what and why we attract certain things into our life.

How Does a Dream Explain Something Before it Happens?

This is your intuition working during your sleep. During your awake time you generally work and are taught nothing but ego and so through time you have learned to deny your intuition that supplies you with insight whether you are sleeping or not.

There are many theories about our sleep. It is my understanding that when we are asleep, we experience our true selves as spiritual beings. We have hundreds of thousands of dreams, but we remember only a hand full. This handful helps us really awaken to the possibilities of our past lives and our future life.

Our spiritual lives are already designed before we arrive on this planet. We have chosen our life plan in advance and our spirit guides help us get back on track and therefore they assist us through our dreams. They help us with spiritual signs that can trigger a dream of a situation that may be coming around the next corner or they can set a thought in motion for you to discover what deters or helps you make the right decision in order for you to remain on your life path.

Often when someone dreams of a situation that has nothing to do with them in ego does in fact have something to do with them in spirit. For example, say you dream of an accident about another person and the next day you meet that person for the first time, would you say something to them right then and there? Or would you say nothing and allow them to be hurt? It is a learning lesson for both of you. First, your learning lesson was to say something to the stranger and second for the stranger to listen to your insight.

This is where ego has killed the spirit. Ego dictates that if you say something so off the wall to another that you are considered to be insane. And yet you're the sane one and you just had an experience of divine guidance.

Now let's say that you did say something to this person and that person actually listened to your guidance and lived to tell the day. Then wow, spirit was successful and so were you and so was the recipient. In this case all of you learned the lessons of the day.

It is not always true that someone won't get hurt in a lesson. However, it is important that you remember that people have many lessons to learn and you cannot judge how they will learn these lessons.

So don't be afraid to learn lessons and don't be afraid to experience your dreams as one day they may indeed save lives and you will be the one who will receive the recognition for it.

Can an angel really show themself to me?

Yes, they most certainly can. However, spiritual beings like angels will not show themselves if it will cause you any kind of harm. The only way an angel or other form of spirit would show itself to you is if you requested this to happen through your own records or if you have earned the right to see them. This earned right would depend upon your studies of Intuitive Arts whether you're with The World Academy of Intuitive Arts or another professional instruction. When you apply yourself to instruction of Intuition then you open the doors for many wonderful new and exciting experiences to take place. You learn by each and every experience.

I have a friend who can read and see angels. She is very experienced. However, it is very difficult for her to see spirit guides or other forms of spirit that are not on the same or similar vibration of angels. She is very good with her respect for such beautiful beings and they are in turn very respectful of her.

No this doesn't mean that if you're a child that has experienced angels that you would have to go to school to learn them. But, I would recommend that you, as the gifted child, seek out the professionals and learn from them as they will teach you many wonderful things about working with angels. In fact, there are many books about angels on the market these days and most are excellent with knowledge of these wonderful spiritual beings.

If you see an angel it is best to say hello. God sends all angels. Some of them appear as feminine and other masculine but all of them are androgynous and do not reside in gender. It is our perception that assigns gender to them. Remember, an angel will mirror your thoughts and they can read your thoughts, so keep them pure and honest.

Now, there have been millions of reports of angels helping people out in time of need, such as an accident. This is pure truth. Angels are not just something out of a comic book or the movies, they are real beings of intelligence and they're made up of white light. The intelligence is the operating factor of the white light being.

Don't be surprised if you see a spiritual sign and it resembles an Angel, such as a cloud formation or an image in the water. These are very good signs that you are being watched over and protected spiritually.

Now, there are millions of angels and so you may, when asking for assistance, receive several hundred at a time and depending on the complexity of the situation you may even wind up with many higher vibration beings like Mother God or Father God or Ascended Masters.

It is important to remember that Angels are here to assist us with our life plans and to assist our spirit guides as well. So never fear an Angel as they show their unconditional love for each and every one of us.

What does a Billboard have to do with it?

Well, simply put, billboards hold information. Right? Well, at least in our physical life they do. However, in spirit they are great forms of information easily spotted by the eye of the aspirant.

If you ask a question and you are driving down the highway more than likely your answer will appear on a billboard. The complexities are your thoughts and those thoughts first have to come from you. You then have to give the intended thought a short amount of time to take effect within your space, time, and plane. You must start to let go and allow yourself to look as directed by spirit instead of intentionally looking for signs. Then the signs will appear to you in a different light.

This works with billboards beautifully, but you can use this type of question and answer with thousands of signs all over the place. Such as license plates and Make and Model of the cars around you. I find that when I practice this type of Q&A. I ask for really big signs that even I couldn't miss and nine times out of ten I find trucks and trailers that display larger signs. Works good for me!

I always say to my students, practice. Try and you will be surprised at the end results and don't be surprised if an abundance of signs come through for you. Our guides want to make contact with us and they try very hard to do so. You will find that when asking for assistance it comes in a greater amount. But, just as I mentioned above it takes practice to learn what your triggers are and to learn how to best ask spirit for help. And on the other hand if you don't try you haven't gained anything, but you may have lost out on the potential to know more.

NOTES

The truth you believe and cling to makes you unavailable to hear anything new.

Pema Chodrun

Understanding Spiritual Signs

What are spiritual signs? Well, they are signs that comes to you through an alternative thought, feeling, vision and/or experience.

This can be a difficult task or it can be easy to learn. It is really up to you. Spiritual signs can be everything around you. It can be the lamp that flickers or the news flash on TV, and it's the roadblocks and construction on your path of travel. It involves your timing with everything that you do. In fact, everything can be a spiritual sign.

Let's break this down into terms we all can understand. You are in need of a new car, then you would say in a question to spirit through your minds intentional thought patterns, I would like to see my new car, I want it to be blue, and have stylish rims and be a convertible. You give this thought just a matter of minutes for the translation to follow through to the Universal Consciousness and Wham! On a cargo truck you see the one. Your new car! It is that easy. You say, no it isn't. Well ok, let us talk about a smaller example.

You're thinking of that new pair of pants. Suddenly you see an advertisement for the pants that you want. There is someone walking by with the very same pants on! This is abundance flowing to your thought or question.

Still not believing this? Think about it this way; have you ever been driving around and wondered if you could get that special parking space? You know the one right by the front door that isn't handicap? You have put out to the Universe that you would like this space and what happens? A space opens up! Wow, now that is cool, you say and you go on about your business after you take the space of course.

Have you ever been walking down the sidewalk and happened to look down and see a water main cover with a rose on it. And then you just happen to look back up and see a truck pass by with a red rose on the side of it. You see a store with the most beautiful roses in the window. This is spiritual abundance working at its best. See you attracted the roses to you and then you where given a chance to see them with your own eyes.

These are of course simple explanations of spiritual signs.

Intense signs may be like these examples:

- Have you ever changed your course in driving for no apparent reason only to find out that there was a major accident in the place you would have been?

- Have you ever been walking home at night and found yourself walking on the other side of the street for no apparent reason, and then you found out the next day that somebody else was stabbed in the very same place that you would have been?

- Have you ever had a gut feeling that something was about to happen and then you advised the others around you to prepare, and there is an earthquake?

- Have you ever had one of those really gut wrenching nightmares on your Elm Street only to find out the next week it really happened?

These examples are taken from students in all walks of life. Each one of them was initially shocked to experience such a things. They said, they didn't think they had it in them. Well everyone does.

Spiritual signs are all around us. We have to be listening or thinking about them in order for our feeble minds to catch them. Or we simply have to ask the question and wait for the answers.

Can a Person be a spiritual sign?

Of course they can. We have Reverends, Mothers and Fathers of the church, Pastor, and even Clergy and each one of them are flesh and blood just as you and I are and they have the ability to be a spiritual sign for you and you for them. Life doesn't stop at the doors of a church.

Any person or being on this planet can be a spiritual sign. There is an experience that talks about spirit speaking through others. This too is a spiritual sign. Although, it takes a skilled person to really listen. Sometimes you're skills allow you to hear the words from spirit that do not match those of the person speaking them. This is when you know that you were hearing an Ascended Master or spirit guide speak as a spiritual sign.

Have you ever experienced a voice in your ear? This would be your spirit guide stating your name or a thought that you needed to hear. This too is a spiritual sign.

Have you ever set your keys down in one place and found them in another later on? (And you don't have anyone living with you that would have moved them.) This is a spiritual sign.

Have you ever seen a ghost or felt the presence of someone near you?

We can go on for pages and pages of documented spiritual signs, but I think you have the point now.

There is no reason to fear such signs as they are there as a help to you.

Have you ever stopped and thought for a moment to think of how the ghost may feel or how the relentless spirit guide is doing? No, and why is that?

We have been taught that life stops or ends after we die and if this were true then why do we have ghosts and spirits? You have to stop and think on how to answer that truthfully. We have them around us because life doesn't end when, life continues when our physical body fails. The soul moves from the body into its truest form the spirit. We are actually spirit incumbent! We are locked into a body for learning purposes and we have guides that lead us on our life path relentlessly. They speak to us every way we are willing to listen.

Spirit speaks through others on a regular basis and it is up to us to develop the skills to learn how to listen carefully. Today we are getting much needed skill level development and are lucky as it is now become readily available to us. So don't wait another minute, learn to listen!

If you have a kitty, have you noticed when you're sad you simply can't get that kitty to leave you alone. The kitty will use a special kind of spiritual signs it is called unconditional love and then he/she will move into position to ease your pains.

Many different types of spiritual signs are at work in our day-to-day lives and all we need do is open our eyes and look a little deeper to see them all around us.

I believe in Divine Intervention. This is something that occurs when we pray for help. I also believe that the Creator sees the workings of our hearts. In this way our good intentions are noticed.

It is always The Intention that matters.

Alison Stormwolf

Divine Intervention

Calling upon Divine Intervention is one way you can really get assistance without joining the next cult or religious order!

The Do's and Dont's

What are the do's and dont's of calling upon the Divine Intervention?

DONT'S

1. Don't expect anything in return.

2. Don't imply danger upon another.

3. Don't ask for something that will only personally gratify your ego.

4. Don't rely on one modality.

5. Don't believe in everything that you see with your physical eyes (illusion).

6. Don't rely on self-pity.

7. Don't rely on others self-pity.

8. Don't rely on one religious view to gratify your own beliefs.

9. Don't follow only one person's training.

10. Don't allow yourself to be mislead.

DO'S

1. Do ask for assistance by allowing the spirited ones to assist you.

2. Do apply unconditional love to others at all times.

3. Do ask for selfless gratification to assist with others.

4. Do rely on multiply modalities to heal yourself and others.

5. Do believe in your feelings through your heart and others chakras (Reality).

6. Do rely on selflessness.

7. Do rely on others selflessness.

8. Do rely on many different points of view in spirituality.

9. Do follow as many persons training as possible, never stop learning.

10. Do inform yourself of the truths around you.

It isn't one idea or practice that leads us away from the truth of our own life path, but is the illusion of our ego will that takes and derails us from the truth of ourselves. There are many services in the world today that can lead us to new and exciting paths in the evolvement of humankind. We are no longer held to the tradition of slavery to each other. Salvation resides in our consciousness, you are your own Messiah. The reason is simple. You're only flipping a light switch from negative to positive thinking, from conditional to unconditional love.

The do's and dont's are only a small fraction of this change and it is really up to you as The Next Messiah to change. In the simplest of terms, either you stay frustrated and watch the world as you know it end, or you can continue on with the world in a positive light.

How hard would it be for you to see your neighbor or your friends go from their struggles to a positive life. We have been facing our true life paths and growing faster and smoother than ever thought possible.

We don't have to wait for a catastrophe where we lose thousands of lives to the selfishness of one, two, or a group waging war against another country or group of people.

For example, do we place a traffic light where it needs to be before the accident or after? Well, after the accident has taken many lives.

Why not place the traffic light in this place before the accident can happen, then you save lives through selflessness. This is a direct positive action.

This makes sense!

The same applies with WAR. What part of taking someone else's life makes any sense for the greed of a county?

Do live life! Don't destroy it!

How it really works

Calling Upon Divine Intervention is a little bit tricky. There are guidelines to follow. These guidelines will help you to call for a deity's assistance in any situation. The tricky part is our unconscious mind. This part of our mind is our power source. You must be clear about your intentions in order for this part of your mind to get the message right. This is where thousands of people make their mistakes when calling upon divine intervention.

Here are the basic guidelines to start:

1. Take five deep and very slow breaths. (Now, if you have some lite headedness, relax and speed your breathing up just a bit, or breathe as you would normally.)

2. Relax and shake off the business of your day. You are about to call on the Divine, so just simply take a break.

3. Align with your thoughts.

4. Sit comfortable in a chair with your feet placed on the ground without shoes on.

5. Place your hands together as if you're about to pray then place them comfortably between your legs or on your lap.

6. Remember this is not a stressful experience.

7. Call to your angels by simply saying, I give my angels permission to assist me.

8. Wait for about a minute.

9. Note any changes in the room's temperature and how you feel. (These will be helpful to you in the future.)

10. Now, call to the angels and ask them to surround you in white light.

11. Ask the angels to shield you from negativity.

12. Now, call to the deity of your choice for assistance.

13. Once you feel this deity's presence, state your request.

14. Ask the deity if they have any messages for you. (Listen, you may feel something, smell something, hear something, our just know something.)

15. Make a note of it.

16. Ask another question or request something in the positive to happen to you or your loved ones.

17. Repeat and ask for the messages.

18. If a time goes by and you don't get a message it means that you will receive one in a different format.

19. Then say thank you for your assistance and thank the angels for clearing the path for you.

20. You're done.

Now if you didn't get anything while you followed this guide then you need to keep your eyes and your ears opened. You're more advanced than you think. You will see an answer somewhere unexpected such as a sign on a billboard, or a cloud form, or a license plate. Look around you. The signs are everywhere.

If you don't see these signs don't give up. It means that you have some blockages and you will want to see several different professionals or take some workshops to learn how to clear these blockages on your own.

Remember, working with a variety of modalities you can clear you life path yourself, you just have to learn. When you learn a modality you pay once and you get to work with for as long as you wish for no additional charge.

For instance Reiki Healing Practioners, is a weekend course. You pay once and yet once you have received you attunements you're on our own. You own what you have learned. Reiki is often used in emergency rooms and hospitals. Harvard School of Nursing teaches first year nursing candidates Reiki. There are many hospitals that offer Reiki through Certified Practioner's, so it is only a matter of time for others to get caught up to the newer healing modalities in the market place today.

Don't ask for more than you can chew

I always say to my students and clients "Don't Ask for more Than You Can Chew". It is true though, as we are creatures of habit to ask for more than we can handle. However, in spirit sometimes that can really bite you in the ass! Spirit works with abundance and so you may ask for a client or two and spirit will send you the world. You can ask for one package of M&M's. But, you didn't stipulate the size and spirit works with abundance, and so you receive the biggest size package you could imagine.

Just as you ask for an angel, you will receive hundreds of angels for assistance. It is important that you stipulate just how much you want and what size and capacity. Once you ask for assistance, you have the infinite universe to answer your request.

Some will pray for rain and then they will ask for Divine Intervention. However, did they ask for a cup of rain or a flood? And, what happens? A flood comes. Everyone says they are being punished and yet they received just what they asked for.

See spirit wants to communicate with us and they are willing to go the mile to assist those of you whom are willing to make the move to communicate with them. When requesting Divine Intervention it is best to indicate exactly what you are asking for.

For example; I knew a fellow that was in need of Divine Intervention. He was being prosecuted for a crime he did not commit. He was in the wrong place and the wrong time. He called through prayer and writing mantras for Divine Intervention. He spent every day for three months asking for this assistance and finally on the day of trail he felt the angels come and assist him. It was amazing. He worked hard and his attorney did too. There were tremendous holes in the investigation and lack of evidence. The police officer believed he could beyond a shadow of doubt sentence this man to jail for the rest of his life.

Three days of trail and three hours of deliberation the twelve jurors and one judge stated unanimously that the man was clearly not guilty of the crime in which he was being prosecuted.

Now, had the man not called upon Divine Intervention to prove the truth, he would be in jail for a crime he didn't commit for the rest of his life and the people who put him there would suffer negative karma for the rest of their lives. You can clearly see how Divine Intervention is a powerful tool indeed.

What does Divine Intervention mean?

Well in the physical life it is described as a Holy Order, a church, The Holy Father, the Holy Mother, Mother Mary, Mother Theresa, God like characteristic of or befitting a deity, extremely good.

However, in spiritual reality it is a prayer to our Holy Father and/or Holy Mother, asking for higher assistance and a request for change to our future for the better good.

It is in the simplest of terms a cry for hope and joy. If you find yourself in dire need then this is the best way to connect for an important resolve. It is important to mention that you really need to do this for the better good and for no harm.

How can I apply for Divine Intervention in my life

You don't apply like a job application! You literally need to look at all your situations and decide which is best to work on first. For example; you have back taxes and you need help with finding the right tax attorney. You could request in writing to the Divine by stipulating "I need help finding the right attorney for my needs". Then you would light a white candle and burn the paper that you just wrote on. I would do this for three days straight and on the fourth day look for signs that would tell you of a tax attorney.

I always say start small, with something that you know and test the waters. You will surprise yourself.

I'll bet that as you leave the house and head to work or the store that you will see a billboard or a sign that indicates so and so is your best bet. Your answer has come to you via a spiritual sign.

Thusly, if you have an athletic side to you and you have a meet coming up, write the letter and burn it through the white candle at least five days in advance. Mind you, you still need to practice and work out, but I'll bet that you will either win the match or win the game. Try it. You won't be disappointed. And should you fail, try to look at how you worded the writings. You may not have failed in writing it, but the energy for the writings was applied elsewhere. This isn't too uncommon, but we are creatures of habit and so you must try again.

Perhaps as a parent you have a child that isn't up to par with their studies. Write the words and burn them with the candle and make sure that you stipulate that this is for you child. A parent's compassion for a child is very strong in the spirit world and therefore you can fight for them until they become of age as mankind stipulates.

Now be looking for an answer. However, never for any reason be expecting and outcome or answer. Selfishness doesn't play well with spirit and it will not be rewarded with anything of value. It is best not to try to figure out what the outcome should be, better to allow spirit to show you the outcome through pictures and small messages if you ask the question.

Here are some other ways to apply Divine Intervention that you may want to think about.

Often times we ask God to assist our loved ones with an illness or comfort them when they are dying. You can write to God-Divine and ask for angels to come and assist them. Every question is answered either with the answer we were looking for in the first place of one that we don't want to hear. However, it important not to blame ourselves for the loss of another and/ or their situation. It is best to help them over by asking for the assistance and then letting them go if need be. You cannot help others if you hold onto them so tightly that you hinder their progression in this dimension or in the next. Remember we all have the right to pass in our own time at our own choice. If you let go of them then you can let them pass completely. This is the best way for a person to return with the Divine assistance that you asked for in the first place.

Another way for Divine Intervention to work is by asking to help an animal or tree. It isn't so uncommon for us to pray for the road kill we see from time to time, I ask for their souls to travel to the Divine with peace and for their physical bodies to become food for those that need it.

This is a way to help both in a positive manner and without regret, known as no harm to all. This statement is very powerful and when applied to a situation the outcome can be very powerful indeed. It is best to stipulate no harm to all and for the better good of all at the end of your requests as this will show to the Divine that you really mean well. And another thought, if you do harm to another through this method, if you request the harm to be done, this will harm you. The karma back flash from such harm can be brutal and fast. This is not recommend for anyone.

When applied with a positive review and a positive outcome the beauty of it really does show in all that you touch. You will feel it too.

Do I have to be religious for this to work for me?

 No, you don't. Though contrary to popular belief, those who are religious can in fact be very spiritual! They chose not to acknowledge their spirituality as they are afraid of being judged by their peers. Once again, fear rules the day over humanities beliefs. It is really quite sad that as a people we have forgotten that we are strong and we can learn and teach ourselves how to do anything. And yet, we allow others within our race to create fear for us.

When you stop and think about it, I mean really think about it, we are powerful in our own right and it is truly sad when you think that our powerful ways have been taken away from us by our own doing!

We are spiritual by birth and religious by choice. When you choose to take back your power in spirituality you chose to return home to spirit. Religions over time have separated you from your own spirit (soul). Now is the time to take back your soul and live as we once did many thousands of years ago when life was once wondrous and full of joy and learning wasn't about fear, but unconditional love.

I empower you to take back your life, to take back your power of soul, to take control and truly live with honesty, truth, and unconditional love, compassion, and thought to live without fear is to live within spirit, "Yourself"!

Ask and you shall receive

Wow, is this a confusing thought. I use to think it was just that easy and yet I tried for years to Ask and Receive. Instead, I received frustration, guilt, and anger. I became angrier about my life and that others had it so much easier.

I learned how to change my trained mind set from ego will surrender to the will of Truth/God. Not an easy task coming from a highly political family that believed in marriage not for love, but for appearances, and that you had to have 2.5 children because that is what your parents did and you had to do the same in order to be appropriate in life. I asked for years to be saved from this family of losses and all I received was more loss. I never understood why until now.

See, if we request for loss to leave us and our intention is centered on the loss, we receive more loss. If we ask to gain better happiness in our lives then we attract better happiness. I never learned that in school. In fact, I never learned much in school because I was one of those kids that was considered a slow learner. However, in fact, I was a very fast learner and the school system was just flat boring!

As I built up my skill level development I learned how to Ask and Receive exactly what I wanted. Not what others thought I should have, but what I really wanted? I wanted to learn, more and more and I'm still like this today.

I'm now 42 years old and I love to learn, I can't seem to learn enough. The reason for this is there are not enough teachers in this world that are trained in teaching the gifted. And the schools are not designed as of yet to teach you the basics of Ask and you shall Receive. In order for you to receive what you are asking for you must think, feel, picture, and love the thought that you're asking for. It seems simple enough, but we fear far better than we love. Our minds go to fear first and then we fight with ourselves to get what we want. By the time we realize what we have done, we have lost the thought of good positive energy to a negative thought. It is the most frustrating event in one's life.

The good news is, we are creatures of habit and if we continue to practice we will receive what we asked for and with abundance. It takes time because we have been taught to fear to get what we want rather than to love what we want in order to receive.

White Candle as a Catalyst

When calling upon Divine Intervention it is important to call in the angels first to set the pace for positive energy flow. White candles are the base for this positive energy flow.

In every church that has been around for centuries past they have always called upon Divine light through the use of white candles. Why is that, you say? White is known as the purist of colors. If you see angels, then you see white and blue colors. If you see ghosts, they usually follow with a white mist. If you see spirits, you may also see white mist.

Think about what you feel, when you see something white! You may feel fresh, clean, and healthy. It is one of the easiest colors to clean and purify both in the physical realm and the spiritual realm.

Still lost on the subject? Well look at it this way. Think of your white car and how you can't stand to see it dirty, so you clean it and suddenly it changes from negative dirt to positive clean. You washed away the negative energy that changed the environment in which you drive. Now your car will run better and get slightly better fuel efficiency. You become happy again and thus lighter in spirit. All is good and is wrapped around your white vehicle.

Now, think about this a little further, if you want to clean out your negative energies around your person such as, always being late or having unusual things happen that delay you in some way. Then get your white candle out light it, call in the angels by saying, "I welcome your assistance angels." Then sit and write about your negativity. When you're done and you feel that you have nothing else to write then write how you would like this to turn out. And when you finish with that then write about your lessons learned. Then read the entire writings out loud and then burn the letter so that Mother God may assist you with your outcome.

Having completed such a ritual I didn't realize the effect it would have on my life. I was desperate to have a positive change in my life. I performed such a task for several weeks over three months and the end result is who I am today. A loving, living spirit within a physical body, learning just as we all do when we choose this Eden for our life paths.

Give yourself the chance to expand and grow with a white candle as you rest at night or as you request Divine Intervention. You won't be disappointed if you try. Set your sights on something small as first and then go for it!

NOTES

The mantra becomes one's staff of life and carries one through every ordeal. Each repetition has a new meaning, carrying you nearer and nearer to God."

Mahatma Gandhi

Mantras

What is a mantra?

A mantra, in Hinduism, is a sacred verbal formula repeated in prayer or meditation. It is a chant or calling to the divine. A mantra is a sacred writing, which is verbally scribed to deities.

This sacred writing is sacred because you write about yourself in a very intimate manner. This intimate manner is not shared with others it is only shared with the deity that you wish to review the mantra.

A mantra is another form of calling upon Divine Intervention. However, this can be a preformed scribe from ancients past or a form of writing that you just wrote today.

The important issue is that you repeat it several times. You do not burn the mantra. The power of a mantra is in the verbal scribe as you speak it, as you feel it, as you vibrate with it. It is in every manner in which you chose to allow yourself to be heard through the fog of the physical body and lessons of life learned through the teachings of earth.

The reality of this mantra can be heard through all vibrations and through all time if perform well.

A mantra is not a toy and it isn't something to be taken lightly. Once you have created a mantra and you relax yourself into a meditative state (yet remain alert) repeat the mantra several times a day or week . It becomes and very powerful life changing tool that will carry you through time itself.

Now be warned, a mantra is a neutral base tool for communicating with the Divine or deities. If used for the better good of all and without harm to all, the outcome is incredibly good. If used in a harmful manner the outcome for you will be dreadful and very difficult to remove. The reason it is difficult to remove is because you would have used your right to free will to create it. Your right to free will is a sacred contract with the Divine and you have the right to change anything you wish in your Life Path. If you change it for the good then all is good, if you change it for the worse then all is worse. The universe doesn't choose what you want, it only mirrors what you want. If you want something good in your life then write and practice a good mantra.

Now, let us talk about what happens when you take matters into your own hands regarding a situation that has nothing to do with you directly. You write the mantra to read something like the following: "I want only the best for my friend, he deserves to be free! I want only the best for his family. I want him to not suffer anymore and I want him to be happy. I don't want him to suffer through this regrettable situation. If, I could I would suffer for him."

Taking on the responsibility of others is not a good idea. The mantra is a powerful tool that will transfer the negative karma to you from him. And you will suffer cruelly, by your own right to free will.

Each of us has chosen to experience various events in our lives. These decisions were made prior to arriving in this life. With this in mind you can still write a mantra of healing for the individual without taking on any responsibility of karma as your own. For example: "I wish for the highest good and with no harm to all that my friend recovers from this experience all the good in it. I wish for only the highest good for him and I will stand by him without harm to me".

This will allow you to support your friend and you won't receive any negative karma for it.

Writing a mantra

Writing a mantra is simple.

1. Find a place in your home, fields, woods, or by the water.

2. Relax. It is important to really relax or do a simple meditation to relax.

3. Make sure to have a pen or pencil and a pad of paper to write with or if you're a computer nut then use your computer.

4. Sit and relax. Find a comfortable position to sit in.

5. Now, start to write with "I wish for the highest good and with no harm to all" then state what it is that you're asking Divine assistance with.

6. Make sure that you intentions are very clear.

7. Now reread the mantra several times over.

8. Now, you're ready to set the schedule for reading you mantra, repeatedly.

9. Once your schedule is set, you need to speak the mantra in a very direct manner. If your mantra is something emotional then you need to feel that emotion.

10. If your mantra is something physical, speak in a really good manner then feel that good emotion. Remember emotion is a driving factor in your Mantra.

11. Now you can apply Emotion and speech to your Mantra for a much more powerful experience.

12. Remember to be consistent with reading your mantra.

13. Set the days needed, such as, if you're trying to assist a patient with cancer then read the mantra for the duration of their stay. If you're helping a friend get through a crisis such as a break up then read the mantra for a week. You will learn to know how long or how short to work with your mantra.

Take your time and practice, practice, and practice. Remember we are creatures of habit and ritual, you will remember how writing a mantra becomes a powerful tool.

A person is involved in a crime and you feel absolutely horrible about it and wish to break free of the punishments that afford such a crime. In today's world you would hire an attorney and you would pay dearly for that criminal defense attorney in the sum of $10,000.00 to $$$$$$$$$ dollars.

Now, in addition, imagine writing a mantra and reciting this mantra over a small period of time like three months for a misdemeanor and maybe six months for a felony. And in this mantra, you write about what you did. The body of the mantra is about the details of your actions. It is important that you describe in detail what you have done. This is not something that you will give away, but the detail of what you experienced is what gives your Mantra power!

Now, with the body of the Mantra written you now need to explain what you learned, not what you fear, but what you have learned from this experience. Did you learn to grow from this experience so that you never need to live it again or do you have more learning to do. This is where you would write about those thoughts and feelings. Remember your feelings drive a very powerful thought.

Now, you have your body of your mantra and you have your lessons of your mantra, it is important to now have your remorse, empathy, and compassion for the other in this situation. Always remembering that the other person involved, volunteered to assist you with your growth. It is equally important to be compassionate, remorseful and have great empathy for the other as they too are learning from this experience that you volunteered for as well!

Now it is time to add the tone of your voice and the feeling to your mantra. See it is great that you have taken the time to write down you subject with still greater detail and your lessons, but it also equally important to write down how your emotions are allowing yourself to feel them. Speak the words as well as read your mantra to yourself and see if it really feels like what you have experienced. Remember to give yourself space and time to write this most important mantra. Remember this will help save you from the illusion of the senses.

This is designed to release you such as you will never have to experience it again.

Some of us experience the same old things repeatedly until we are blue in the face and we never learn. This is a time for completion. We must do the best that we can. Having so many wonderful inspirational teachers all around us today helps to give us this newly founded way of completing our learning cycles with less time involved and more learning.

Your mantra should be spoken with great love and energy to prove that you are past the training. And that you feel the remorse and empathy for the other and understand that your speech and emotions should reflect how you truly feel. Not what ego tells you what to feel. Spirit doesn't respond to falsities, only Truth!

Now you will want to read your mantra every day! After reading your mantra asked to be released from this responsibility or learning, so that you may move on in a positive nature in your life.

After you have spent the time you believe to be needed to accomplish your goals then ask for Divine Intervention and light a white candle and burn your mantra!

Comparing a mantra to other healing methods

I have known plenty of powerful people in my day some known as skilled intuitives, psychics, doctors, PhD's, and Psychologists. It always amazes me how these skilled and educated individuals never, or very rarely, look at the truth to any given situation, just at the symptoms!

A symptom can be healed for a relatively short time, but is not the cure of the causer. Our health care systems today aren't geared up to cure the causes only the symptoms.

A mantra can be used in repetition with regard to reminding one's self that you can in fact ward off dis-ease and dis-orders. The mantra is a series of words formed into sentences that can be formulated to ones needs only or to a group or to summons any being. This in itself is very powerful. It is best when one can learn to heal one's self rather than continue inappropriate health care. We are not saying that all health care is inappropriate however, when it becomes redundant or continual then it is.

Mantras are considered to be the long form version of healing modalities. It takes a skilled mind to create and perform the mantra and it takes time and patience. For the same results to take place, you may choose a form such as Reiki. Reiki is performed by the laying of hands and the sessions can last as long as the practioner can handle it. However, with Reiki you need to see a practioner. With a mantra you are the practioner.

We are creatures of habit and we like to take our time learning and performing. The longer you practice the better the performance.

This is not to discourage those interested in self-mantras, but it is necessary to inform you of the truths.

If you are not trained in writing a mantra and you learn from a book it will take you about 2 years to see decent results from you work. Now, should you see a Reiki Practioner that is skilled through Mastery level it would take you about a half hour to see such the same results.

It is important that you remember the Mastery level of Reiki took the practioner about two years to learn and practice at. This is why we say a Mantra is a powerful tool. Once you have learned it you own it for life.

Do you really have the power to help others or yourself? Absolutely!

It is important not to get yourself overwhelmed when studying any healing modality. We need our time to study, learn, and practice. It is always a good idea to practice at any level alone and with others. What is more important though is working with individuals that are brutally honest with you.

We say yes, because we are all the same, now some of us will fight and say no that we are not all the same. However, we are and we are all from the same stock to boot. In other words, we all have souls and we all bleed red blood. We all have to work at something and we all need to drink water, and breathe air.

We all have the ability to heal our self and others. Like with anything, we have to remember to do the work to learn or to unlearn. We have to remember that this isn't our first time here and that we can do everything from memory or just by simply asking for the help.

For instance, if you're lost anywhere and you don't have directions what do you do? Well, you stop and ask for help and you find out what the right directions are. This is equally true about life. Say you need to learn how to build a home. Well then, you will go to a college or vocational school and learn the trades necessary for you to do so.

Say you want to become a medical practioner, well then you will go to a school that teaches you the exact practice you wish to learn. This greatly reduces the learning time. All-in-all you are able to do miraculous healings on yourself and others, you just have to remember how to do so and practice so that one day you can heal yourself and others.

Difference of mantras through time

Mantras, through the ages, have been built on the concept of sounds, words or groups of words that are considered capable of creating spiritual transformation as well as physical transformations. Their uses and types vary according to the philosophy or the religion associated with the mantra.

For example:

If you where a Hindu in previous centuries you would have followed a religious orders mantra for every type of need possible.

If you where a tribal leader such as a Chief, or Shaman you would have followed the history of your ancestors philosophy in a mantra and dance for rain or for food.

If you follow a religion you would follow your Pastor or Reverend in a ritual song and prayer.

You would have always followed the words or group of words that related to your situation.

Through time from the cave man to the current day Vatican we all share very similar traits in our day-to-day rituals that follow a mantra.

Some say that a mantra only applies to those of either Hinduism or Buddhism, but this just simply isn't true. In every book and every document that you've read; in every word lays a mantra.

There are those that state the word Aum. Aum is in itself a mantra. Aum is a word that means Father God, or God Consciousness, it also is the sound of the white light and the sound of shifting in our Consciousness. It means all these things and much more and yet it is just a word.

Some state that if you practice Aum then you will become one with the Father (God). Many people's practice in meditation with Aum and lift themselves to a much higher vibration. Aum also brings us peace and joy, it can quite the mind and expand the soul. So, you see there are many reasons to practice a word!

Now it isn't to say that your mantra should be just one word. We are human beings and if you live in the United States of America you will use many words to describe your mantra meaning. However, if you live in China or Japan and many other Asian societies you will find the one word that describes your needs.

See we all come from many walks of life and through generations we continue to evolve and with a little help here and there a mantra can be your success!

Mantras in WICCA and the Christian Bible

WICCA

Even though mantras have been thought of as belonging to Buddhism and Hinduism it is common to find hundreds of thousands of mantras within Wiccan traditions.

Most Wiccan traditions follow a book or diary of mantras that represent various spells, incantations, and a special code. Wicca also follows a deity known as a Goddess and Horned God and they practice by many different rituals that review words just as a mantra does.

The Christian Bible

The Christian Bible is a form of a very powerful mantra. Every Sunday you will find that the Bible in one form or another is preached or sermoned to the people with songs and written in true mantra fashion. The repeating of these songs and words (pray and liturgy) allows fellowship and you find human friendship and companionship. It is a way for humankind to feel a part of something greater than one's self.

Here is the Jesus Prayer (Η Προσευχή του Ιησού) or "The Prayer" (Evkhee, Greek: Η Ευχή - the Wish) is a short prayer or mantra esteemed and advocated within the Easter Orthodox church:

"Lord Jesus Christ, Son of God, have mercy on me, a sinner."

The prayer has been widely taught and discussed throughout the history of the Eastern Churches. It is often repeated continually as a mantra part of personal ascetic practice, its use being an integral part of the eremitic tradition of prayer known as Hesychasm (Greek: ἡσυχάζω, hesychazo, to keep stillness).

The spiritual fathers have a special respect for this prayer. as a method of opening up the heart and bringing about the Prayer of the Heart (Καρδιακή Προσευχή). The Prayer of The Heart is considered to be the Unceasing Prayer that the apostle Paul advocates in the New Testament.

NOTES

Trees are Earth's endless effort to speak to the listening heaven.

Rabindranath Tagore

Listening to Spirit

The concept of listening to spirit is relatively easy. Think about all those you know who have some wonderful and positive experiences in life. There is a good possibility they were listening to spirit.

Just as priests, rabbis, pastors, reverends, nuns and monks all have at least one thing in common, they learned to listen to spirit. Now, you don't have to become a spiritual leader or follower in order to listen to spirit. You just listen.

When a spiritual leader or teacher mentions to you to meditate, what do you think they are asking you to really do? They are asking you to slow down and rest. This allows you hear spirit and receive guidance. It is like having a manual of life in your back pocket. It takes up little space and yet offers you infinite knowledge of everything and everyone. Cool huh!

What people become tied up with is the idea of "Woo-Woo"! Now, I must admit after my parents got through with me everything I do now sounds like what my father would have described as "Woo-Woo" or "crazy". You don't get along in this world focused on others thoughts. This has been one of my biggest learning lessons. I always focused on what others knew and thought and made that mine, then I started to learn that I didn't believe in what they were saying so I decided to listen to my own thoughts and make those my own.

I eventually learned to listen to spirit, it seemed I couldn't try them and fail. Every time I listened to spirit, I was right on the money! However, every time I listened to my parents I never made it out of the barn.

As a young child I found myself, maturing at a high vibration and my parents did not understand what was happening with me. This is common for many children. Their parents do not understand their children's gifts. All children will hide away their gifts rather than get into trouble.

Learning to listen is not as hard as you might think or have been told by others. You already listen, you just don't realize it. Let's take some examples:

1. Say you're driving down the road and suddenly you feel the need to pull off and go a completely different direction than usual. You do so and later learn that a deadly car crash took place just a few miles down the road right where you would have been had you stayed on your course. (You wonder how you knew.)

2. Say you're pulling into a parking lot and you're not exactly feeling well and you think for a moment, "How nice it would be to have the first space in front of the store?" Then suddenly you request comes true and the perfect space opens just as you pull around to it. (You again wonder how this could happen.)

3. Let's say for a moment you press your own clothes and you're meeting with some top executives today. You're in the office typing on the computer and something just "happens to draw your attention" to the right side of your shirt and notice that you forgot to press one sleeve. (You wonder how come you noticed this now and not a couple of days earlier when you actually completed the pressing.)

These three very different examples are very simply explained as your spirit guides guided you through different outcomes and what is very interesting is you listened!

In example number one, you took heed to the situation and followed the inner guidance.

In example number two, you asked for the assistance and it was granted.

In example number three, you simply laughed at the mistake and thanked your spirit guide for the drawing off their attention to keep from experiencing a moment of embarrassment.

In all three examples, the spirit guides where guiding you through your soul's access to intuition. In short, you would be listening to spirit.

How does learning to listen to spirit work?

First you have to be willing to relax. We are trained to run at everything we do. We are not generally trained on how to slow down unless we are a meditation specialist.

So the first thing you have to do is slow yourself down. It isn't easy and it can be very exhausting to try and do so without training from a professional in the field. I would recommend learning how to meditate from someone who meditates on a regular basses.

A Master Teacher would be best to find, but if you simply don't live near one or can't afford the cost to see a Master Teacher then try to meet with a spiritual teacher that can teach you simple meditations.

There is a type of mediation that takes about five minutes to do. When you do them, make sure you are lying down because it will knock you out cold if you have never done a meditation.

See, meditations take time and those who focus their daily activities on spiritual wisdom are the best to learn this process from. Just as with any type of business venture you will need a plan. So set some time aside and plan to work on meditation every day for five minutes and give yourself about ten minutes really.

You need to sit in a quiet place (like your bedroom) and then light a white candle and simply just shut down every part of your body that isn't absolutely necessary. Then you take five deep breaths from your diaphragm and slowly release them. With each breath you take, you will descend into relaxation. However, since your body isn't used to slowing down you will descend into a rest-full sleep. You should wake up within five minutes. If you have more time allow yourself the time to try it again. Remember we are creatures of habit and it takes practice.

Now secondly, you will want to ask a simple question that you don't know the answer to, but can easily find out when researched. This question should be something along the lines of your life. Remember, the first answer that comes to mind in the right answer. A warning – if you second-guess your first answer, you will always prove it wrong. Our logical mind will be in conflict with the part of the mind that dreams and imagines. The conflict can keep you from realizing truth.

Our logical mind, which is the part of mind that does the dramatic imagining will cause conflict with the side of your mind that realizes truth!

Most important is to always remember to relax in any given situation. You cannot listen to spirit if you do not allow this relaxation to take place. Spirit will always try to reach you. If you are not relaxed then you will only receive pieces of the original message and you may get it wrong.

It is important to remember that we are creatures of habit and we must practice in order to get it right with anything that we do. Now, if this comes second nature to you, well then you may be a natural but guaranteed you will need to work at something in your lifetime on Earth.

Ask a question and listen to spirit's answers.

Once relaxed you are ready to ask a question and listen to spirits answers. These answers come in all forms and fashions. It can be a billboard, license plate, in a store, from a friend, in the form of money, on a credit card and anywhere your language is spoken or written.

It is true that sometimes your answers will come to you in a riddle or rhyme, but mostly they will be just a thought in your mind, sometimes making no sense. If you watch in the next day or so you can follow how many times your thought will emerge in sentences and everything around you. Powerful or is it just abundance?

We're a tough creature to get through to sometimes. Abundance plays a very large role in our lives and seems we are always looking. Spirit knows this and so answers us with abundance, not to mention the angels and other high vibration beings love to give with abundance. We can follow a dance of abundance with all things.

Now a more intense type of question. These questions should be about something that you can prove in our space and time. Yet, make the question a bit more intense or descriptive such as, will my marriage survive?

Be ready to look and listen; whenever you're drawn to a picture or listen to audible words from others. Remember, it may happen very quickly or it may take time, it just depends on the person.

Is this person good for my needs and me? Be ready to see the signs that lead you to your answer. They may come in many forms such as on the Internet or on the mirror of your bathroom. his morning, I asked how will my day work out and do I look ok for what I need to do.

The first sign that I saw was my housemates were in unusually good mood. Then I got into my auto and on the floor was a pin that had a sunshine background with a smily face and at the bottom it read "Looking Good Award". Then while I was on my way to work I saw one of my animal spirit guides on top of a lighting pole facing with its back to me. Then I saw a trailer through a chain link fence that read "Cloud 9". These similar happenings are not just by coincidence they are meant to be a form of abundance that I was able to ready myself to receive.
You can do the same.

It isn't by chance that I happen to notice these very important answers to my question, but written by spiritual law. "Ask and you shall receive!"

The "WOW" Factor!

The "WOW" Factor, is a form of realization that one experiences just as they are having a wonderful experience with spirit answering the questions. Sometimes this factor has taken an individual by surprise as they awake from a dream that answered their question or maybe they experience a spirit guide making themselves known to you. This shock value actually derails us from our mission temporarily. Then we try again and again until we get it right. Practice helps us become more efficient in our questions and meditation.

The "WOW" Factor works for me, too. Just because I'm a Master Teacher in this space and time doesn't mean that I too cannot learn and perfect as any other around me. I too am surprised when spirit makes themselves known to me they come in very strong and sometimes will startle me until I realize that they are here to support me or guide me on a new mission of learning. Then I awaken to their vibration and we start working together on a very important project like this book.

It is not uncommon for us to have many spirit guides at given times to assist us with our daily mission of learning and it is very important that you listen and look carefully for all the information that is around you for each mission of learning.

As we are creatures of habit, we need to constantly have recognition for our work and appraisal for our accomplishments. In spirit we receive accomplishments by means of a new spirit guide that comes to assist us with our next project. We can also receive accomplishments with our own lives and living environments by simply living better or getting along better in our environments.

Life becomes easier as the lessons become more intense. It really is up to us to make the changes needed in our lives and not be afraid of moving towards good verses just trying to get what is necessary. See, life will open up for you when you learn to let go.

Clairaudience

Many people have heard in one ear or another a voice and when they turned around no one was physically standing there! Was this real? Did I in fact hear something? Or, am I going crazy? Yes, Yes, and No.

Yes, you did in fact hear your spirit guide(s) speak to you, either to warn you of an upcoming event or just simply reminding that they are alive and well.

Some people have the ability to really communicate in a clairaudient manner. They hear all that is needed from their spirit guides.

Clairaudience is a form of extra-sensory perception where a person acquires information by paranormal auditory means.

Clairaudience is described as follows:

a) A person capable of hearing paranormal activity through sounds to the outer ears (just as a physical person is talking next to you).

b) A person hearing through the inner-mental-ear.

c) Any person that can have their intuitive capabilities alerted to sounds, noises and voices not physically present to others near.

d) Clairaudience is essentially the ability to hear in a paranormal manner, as opposed to paranormal seeing and feeling.

e) Clairaudience may refer, not to actual perception of sound, but may instead indicate impressions of the "inner mental ear" similar to the way many people think words without having auditory impressions.

Now, there are two types of "Clairaudient" people:

First, those who can literally hear voices from the outer ear. Just as surely you were standing next to someone speaking to you or better yet you're listening to a great CD you love and the sound is crystal clear to your ear.

The second is those who can hear voices from the inner ear or the mental ear just as we formulate thoughts in our imaginary mind.So does spirit when we transmit thoughts to the intuitive mind. This is all done inside your head and you literally hear with clarity a voice or multiple voices in your mind.

Nine times out of ten, the physiologist will diagnose a patient with this type of hearing as insane and the diagnoses would be entirely incorrect. The person has a paranormal ability to hear spirit speak. More commonly, you would hear your spirit guide(s) speak to you in this manner without inducing a channeled connection.

All in all we all have the ability to listen if we are willing to take the time to be patient to listen to those that can truly lead us without error!

A moment in time as time stands still

This is best experienced with a master in meditation or as you lay in bed preparing for sleep. Sitting in Nature with the trees and animals, sometimes you can experience this type of phenomenon. Sitting next to a slow flow of water like a small waterfall or stream. focus on the slowly moving water, you can feel the world around you slow down. It will seem like a frame of film at a time moving every minute instead of every second.

We call this phenomenon A Moment in Time, As Time Stands Still.

Focus and staying present elongates time, causes time to stand still.

In larger meditation groups the teachers will bring in birds for focus. They will ask the class to focus on the wings and then slow them down. What actually happens is you slow down your time and so does everything around you.

Suddenly you notice that the wings of the little humming bird have nearly become still. Then shock sets in and you're so completely amazed at yourself that you suddenly start the speed back up and lose that moment in time.

Don't worry, this is true for all of us as we learn how to mold time and understand the principles of it.

One day my best friend and I went for a walk up in the hills around Rowena, Oregon. There is a nice trail which takes you to a vista to see the mighty majestic Columbia River Gorge. It is truly a spectacle to witness. We were hoofing it on this upward trail and when reaching the top we noticed there were a lot of people on the trail below and some at the top. As we turned down the trail we came around a corner and a large rattlesnake was waiting. Normally my best friend would literally freak, but she didn't. She was behind me and I was now looking at the four to five foot snake on the trail with it's five to six inch rattles, shaking with all getup. I froze and then (and this was a part of the moment in time where all stood still) I raised my hands and sent Reiki to the snake Not knowing what else to do, I called in for spiritual help! The snake's rattle simply went limp. I was completely shocked. Then the snake turned and went down the trail in front of us.

As I stood there everything was dead quite (no noise) then I could hear the noise of people talking to my best friend in shock that I was so close to this rattlesnake. I even said to the man down at the next turn back the kids up the snake is coming down the hill (needless to say they scurried back). The snake stopped about four feet down and turned right and stopped on the other side of the path. I followed it and realized that it was stunned as the snake stopped then started to roll sideways down the path. We were all shocked so I said, "Oh, my God! I zapped it!" I stopped the Reiki and the snake slowly started to move up into the foliage. It was simply amazing this ability that I have. After the snake's tail cleared the foliage the snake stopped moving. I think it fell asleep. I stood there while everyone passed and then we continued down the path of the hill. We still talk about that day.

A moment in time isn't just about snakes and other animals, it is an understanding of how we view our lives and ourselves. We need to learn how to slow down and really enjoy our planet and our friends. You cannot experience a moment in time if you don't get out and see the world and the people in it. So, try. You won't let yourself or others down and you may even meet others in the same boat as you.

Angels and their messages for us

People have a preconceived notion that angels aren't spirits! In fact angels are pure spiritual beings of white and other color light. These pure spirits have very specific responsibilities. For example, healing, hope, peace, remembering, joy, singing, play, morals, strength, fertility, justice, fate and love.

There are millions of angel types and they can span over time, space, and dimensions in any given moment. Here are just a few names of different types of angels:

Guardian Angels; Archangels; Cherubim Angels; Seraphim Angels; Powers Angels; Carrions Angels; Virtues Angels; Dominions Angels; Librarian Angels; Akashic Record Angels; Council Justice Angels; Messengers Angels; Grand Hall Angels; Grand Hall Research Angels; Grand Hall Planetary Angels; Kingdom of God Angels; Thrones; Ethers' of God Angels.

The angels live in every one of us and in every being who ever lived or lives! Angels are in all of us, in our cells and in our memories. They can come in a form as a human being, or an animal, or just in person as a spirit or ghostly apparition.

Angels have the ability to manifest in any time and space as well as dimension. In fact, every person who works in the field of the paranormal works with angels to some degree or another.

Without angels we wouldn't be able to survive this world. In short, they really help us through difficult situations that we have no choice but to live, if we let them.

Now, if you wanted to call on an angel you just simply find a peaceful space in your home or work and simply say, "I give my angels permission to assist me in every manner of my life!" That's it. Then be careful and look for the signs and be ready to listen to them answer and assist you through your life. Now, with most of my students they will experience this phenomenon and become excited and then forget how they got there in the first place and then they don't feel the angel again for awhile. This is completely ok. You will learn how to control this excitement and to make it last longer than just a few seconds.

You can also call on the angels for very specific needs as well and I would recommend that you pick up a variety of books telling you about them so you can better understand and familiarize yourself on how to call to your angels.

Let me share a situation with you where I felt the presence of an angel with me.

I used to drive a Motor Coach as a Tour Driver for Grey Line Portland many years ago. I was returning to the bus yard and it was dusk and raining. Exiting the freeway, I turned on a curve to the left. I suddenly saw a sparkle of light over the wheel and I felt like something was wrong so I continued to slow down the bus now cruising about twenty miles an hour through this slow left turn. Suddenly I saw a brown van with its headlights on high coming very fast towards me going the wrong way. All I saw was a very large angel appear before me as if she were standing on the bumper outside and reaching in to the steering wheel and she turned it just enough and she gave full application on the brakes as I came to a stop as the van was now wedged between the bus and the concrete divider.

Afterwards, the police asked, "How did you manage to move the bus over so far?" I said, "It wasn't me. There was an angel on the dashboard. Miraculously, there was a minor scrape at the rear of the bus from the front driver's side mirror on the van. No one was hurt and the van had seven small children in it!

I took pictures as is required in a commercial incident. My supervisor noticed the rear wheels looked like they had slid sideways about four feet. They couldn't explain it, but the tires on the rear wheels where in fact scraped up from sliding sideways that far. In short, my angels came to save me and the individual in the other vehicle. Perhaps you may have a memory or two of these wonderful beings helping you.

Here is another example of how angels look after all of us, especially in very difficult and quick thinking experiences.

I was still with the motor coach company when I experienced a very special moment with many angels.

I was driving a larger 46 passenger motor coach to Mt. Hood Meadows for a day of skiing. I was one of five motor coaches headed up the mountain on that very cold morning. The roads where icy and full of about two feet of packed snow and ice. Not so bad to drive on slowly! I had stopped in Sandy, Oregon to chain up and let my passengers get some coffee and snacks just a few minutes earlier.

Most motor coach operators would stop and chain up much later, but I love safety and I have a perfect driving record because of it. I decided to chain all tires which means; the steer, drive and tag axels. Now, I don't think at the time I was thinking about my intuition, however, I knew the roads were bad and that I didn't want to wind up like other buses, in the ditch.

Now, as my coach climbed up out of Sandy, Oregon heading East on Highway 26 to Government Camp and as we came around "Shorty's Corner" I was traveling about twenty miles an hour and we were on packed snow. I felt the coach slip sideways in the rear for an instance and I corrected it by removing my foot from the accelerator. It was pitch black out and snowing lightly. I decided to slip down the hill side in second gear and just simply touch the brakes every so often to keep the big motor coach from accelerating over ten miles an hour. As I did this I moved the coach into the left lane for more traction in the soft snow. The slow lane was getting too icy to keep continual control.

A small white pickup truck pulling a tandem (two) axle box trailer passed us on the right side moving about thirty miles an hour with his trailer brakes locked up. Not a good sign!

I continued to slow the coach down and as I came down the hill I saw in the oncoming lanes a small four door sedan doing what looked like loop-de-loops. I was completely puzzled and then I realized they were out of control and on ice! I about popped my pants as the entire accident unfolded right before my eyes. The smaller white truck that had passed me had lost control and now was in my lane about a half a mile ahead of me and the smaller car was moving about thirty miles an hour towards him. They struck each other and landed in the ditch to my right. Just before their accident, I told my passengers to brace for an impact at the front of the bus. I didn't think I would live!

The trailer flipped upside down and was now headed towards the front of the bus just to the center of the windshield. I said, "Oh God, help!" Immediately I felt two pairs of hands move my steering wheel to the left just a bit, and the whole bus turned on ice to the left nearly 90 degrees. I felt the wheel turn to my right nearly 120 degrees the opposite way and the bus responded as we literally slipped right around the trailer and both vehicles. Then I felt the steering wheel turn 150 degrees left to lock the front wheels in a hard left turn position. The motor coach slid sideways 436 feet before coming to a stop upright and undamaged. The four motor coaches behind me hit one another in some form or another, but all the passengers were ok.

My passengers, police, paramedics, supervisors and family members were pleased to see that the only people that were injured were in the sedan. There was one more vehicle involved, a double fuel tanker that was sideways just behind my coach. Again, no one injured there either.

The folks in the white pickup truck had an infant in the front seat with them and the baby was still sleeping! Now, this could be called a miracle, but it was the angels that came when I called God for help!

Later on that day when I had all the paper work done for the incident, I was able to take my motor coach up the mountain to pick up my passengers. When I arrived at Mt. Hood Meadows I had a warm welcome from the lodge and all the people involved. I stood in awe of the amount of people applauding me for a successful endeavor. I turned and thanked God for the experience.

My greatest wish is that each and every one of you have the ultimate experience with angels, maybe not in an extreme circumstance as I have, but in a favorable environment.

It is important to know that angels can speak to you through your minds ear or through a voice in your outer ear. They can come to you as a protective bubble in a fire or as a breath of fresh air while in the water. They can come to you while you're sleeping and visit you while you're working.

You know how some people say look at the snow angels and the clouds that look like angels. Yes, it is true, they can come to you that way too. I like looking for signs when I give my angels permission to assist me in a situation. The signs for me are a little bit clearer than for most. I look for signs on billboards, road signs, license plates, numbers and so much more. I look for signs in people too.

Angels are all around us and they love to help us so all we need to do is ask for them or give them permission to assist us in any giving situation.

Have you ever wondered how a friend can finish your sentence.

It just a little thing really, when a friend surprisingly finishes you're sentence. And yet every time it happens people tend to literally freak out or they find it really cool. Why is that?

It is because we have many kindred souls around us. These souls have experienced many lives together. We tend to work with each other time after time to perfection. It is a way of recognizing a person or a pet from a previous lifetime. It gives us comfort and joy to know that we have seen them somewhere else in some other time. It also raises the thought of how can we remember this soul from a different life path. We can take that thought to the depths of time and still never really know how it works. We are a large batch of soul fragments who were born at the same time. And each soul fragment has the ability to hold life in a life path for perfection.

We share many soul fragments with each other's fragments and through time we often come back in touch with those we have met previously. We are also meeting others that we will experience in the future.

I have a best friend and from time-to-time we may share this ability. What happens with us is we have lots of dreams with each other in them. This is a similar experience.

I have shared on numerous occasions a finished sentence or two with friends, and family. Try it so you too will experience the joy in knowing that you're connected in such a manner and then you will realize you're not alone. We are many experiencing this life together as one very large team!

There are an infinite number of universes existing side-by-side and through which our consciousnesses constantly pass. In these universes, all possibilities exist. You are alive in some, long dead in others, and never existed in still others. Many of our "ghosts" could indeed be visions of people going about their business in a parallel universe or another tie – or both.

Paul F. Eno, Faces at the Window

Ghosts

What are ghosts?

Ghosts are a part of a soul or fragments of a soul. Ghosts are pieces of our souls that separated during a traumatic or an unfavorable experience. These Life Paths may not seem traumatic to some of us, however, departing the only thing you remember to be real can be very traumatic.

Ghost's fragments means that you only see some or part of the real soul's appearance in this lifetime. For example, if you were to come across a grumpy ghost or apparition it would mean this ghost has less fragments of its original soul present. It could also be that this fragmented ghost had a traumatic life path and hasn't really left this plain of existence yet. In these types of cases you would then see a ghostly silhouette in form instead of a real shape of a person.

Another example of a ghost not leaving would be the warm friendly energy of a grandmother. She would have wanted to stay for the soul reason of wanting to make sure the home is well provided for.

Ghosts can be plasma based or simply transparent, silhouette, misty, colorful, cold, warm, happy, and/or grumpy.

For example when I was eighteen, my brother called me on the phone and asked me to come back to my parents house to clear a grumpy ghost that he had been experiencing ever since I moved out three years earlier.

My best friend at that time was Darcy and she too was psychic (so was her grandmother). She and I got into my little car and drove to my parent's home. As we arrived, I could feel the energy in the garage, it was very cold. It was freezing in the garage only. We lived in El Cajon, CA at that time. It was late summer the temperature outside was in the high seventies.

As I used my key to enter into the garage the lock unlocked and then the door wouldn't open until I said, "You will clear this door" I used my level of love for my brother as my level of intent for the energy to clear the door. Then the door opened automatically.

As Darcy and I walked into the garage, we could see a silky silhouette or a misty silhouette hanging out by the wall to my brother's room. I walked around two cars parked in the garage and then up to the house door. As I touched the door handle, it was very hot. This was a truly grumpy ghost that wanted only my brother and wasn't about to let me in smoothly. I was a white light soul to this dark spirit ghost and it knew that I meant business. I called in Father God, and asked for the angel's assistance, the door suddenly became cool to touch and it opened smoothly.

The house seemed cooler than normal, but I didn't care. I ran upstairs to the third floor and to my brothers bedroom. As we entered the hallway, the light started to dim and it became really thick or dense air. I knew it wasn't happy to have me there so I increased my intensity of love for my brother's well being and I was able to pass through it without harm.

As I opened the door my brother was hanging from the wall that faced the garage, nearly three feet above his bed, and he was screaming, "Help me!", and, "Let me go! "

As I walked in I said, "You will put him down safely and you will face me now!" Well that ghostly aberration turned and looked right at me and I said, "Do you remember me?" The ghost started to disappear and then I said, "I sent you to Father God by way of the Angels". The ghost was completely gone. My brother jumped of the bed and into my arms and said, thank you. After, Darcy and I went through the entire home. We blessed and cleared away any negativity through the "White light and the Holy Spirit with the help of Father God." We were only in our teens then. My brother didn't have any more problems with nasty ghosts in that house.

I don't want you to think that all Ghosts are nasty, or bad, or mean. When

I was growing up my mother would work all the time at a hospital in New Jersey and we lived about an hour from the hospital. She would leave the house around 4 a.m. and go to work. I was home alone with our five cats, dog, and several wonderful angels and my great grandmother's ghost. We called her GG. When lonely I would go into our vanity in the voyeur and sit in on the toilet just to feel her presence. I would sit there sometimes for hours on end just to be near her. As I got older, I realized that I didn't have to be in the bathroom on the first level I could go up stairs to her bedroom on the third level and feel her there too.

We had a dog named "Flip" he was a beautiful Collie and big of course. I was just four years old. Flip was a warm spirited being that just loved us very much and took good care of my brother and I. When Flip passed away, my father had buried his body in the back yard close to the forest line.

Years later friends would come over while my mother was at work and we would do things like trying to pull on Flip's spirit. Well it worked and it shocked us all. A ball formed right before our eyes and it was incredible, this white light and then I could feel Flip's presence. It was his soul which came through in order for us to see him. I will never forget that wonderful being. He touched my life in every positive way you can imagine. He stayed with me for many years and until I could learn how to free him from this plane. He is now back where he needs to be.

Why do ghosts live among us?

Ghosts live amongst us because they have unfinished business in this existence. This unfinished business we speak of can accommodate many avenues such as:

Ghost not wanting to leave this plane of existence.

Ghost needing to complete a task that can be completed in a ghostly form.

Ghost needing to complete a task that can be completed in a ghostly form on one plane beneath our own.
Ghost departed in a traumatic manner, such as, sudden death from this plane of existence.

Ghost departed in subtle manner and wished to remain to help those around them succeed on their Life Path.

Ghosts are not as they are depicted on TV or in movies. There are many creditable ghosts that work with us all around us every day and you don't even know it. They are a part our lives just as we are a part of their lives. We live in a world that has taught us that we are it. The physical matter that we see with our own eyes is the only existence. This is why Master Teachers like myself are coming forward and being awakened to inform the world through our writings that there is much more to life than just the simple task of being a human being.

Your body has soul, cells, and intelligence, as does your environment and all the individual beings around you.

Ghosts live amongst us because they are achieving their need to perfect and they are helping us to achieve ours. The next time you see or feel a ghost tell them from your heart how much you appreciate their presence so they will know you appreciate them. Remember, they are people just like you, on a different plane of existence one level below our own.

What could we possibly learn from ghosts?

First, we can learn compassion. We have learned that ghosts are here learning too and so we are experiencing their compassion for themselves and us. We can learn through intent that love can pass through time and existence and still maintain a true passion to assist other living beings.

An example:

I live with several ghosts. They appear and disappear in what seems like random times of the day. Or is it random? Their appearance sometimes catches me of guard and then I'm startled. They do this to warn of upcoming events or help me to grow and learn more about them. One of the ghostly forms, as I write, is named Jenifer. She is a young woman who died around her 18th birthday from a violent car accident nearly ten years ago. Now this seems like a long time to us, but in spiritual time, it isn't.

Jenifer and I were friends in life and we are still friends in death. The soul survived the physical being and now exists as a ghostly form. Alive, she was a wonderful and warm being, in death she is a wonderful and warm being. She comes almost every day and I ask her, "Do you want to depart here?", and she says, "No." She feels she is here to help others and so she remains.

In spirit the Hall of Records recognizes this task of remaining to be very good for the soul to perfect and it is recorded as a good mark on ones record. I send all my love to her and ask her to continue helping her family out as she has always done. Soon though she will leave this existence and move on to her next level of work to perfect for the Father God. She is truly a divine being.

So you can see we can learn much in a positive manner from these perfecting souls known today as Ghost's. Are they related to us in some manner?

Yes, however, the manner you may be referring to isn't how they are related to us. In traditional teachings we are taught that what we are handed has been handed down by our physical families and to some degree that is true. However, that is not all that we are. We are much more.

We have a spiritual genealogy just as we have a physical genealogy. In our physical genealogy, we have a mother and a father, siblings, cousins and grandmothers and grandfathers.

In spiritual genealogy we have Father God and we have the feminine principle of Father God, called Mother God, and we are born as a soul. The essence of our being is androgynous. The truth of us, the spirit, is always whole, complete, and perfect. Our soul journey is about our relationship to that we call our creator. Our soul remains whole and perfect in the eyes of the creator. It is our attachment to our beliefs and ego mind, which causes us to seek what we see as human perfection. We were never thrown out of the Garden of Eden and God never abandoned us. It is our own fear and inability to comprehend the creator as infinite, ever evenly present as love. Our search for a soul mate is the search to understand ourselves our heritage as being a child of the creator. When we understand our identity isn't in the physical body or the ego mind, but in our essence, spirit, as a child of the creator we no longer feel split and unfinished.

If a ghost remains by your side for whatever reason you can rest assured that you are working with a kindred soul in the same batch of souls born at the same time. Thusly you are related to them in a spiritual form!

Now, if we take out the spiritual genealogy then you have to focus on why you are encountering this ghostly apparition. Now, if you don't believe in the truths spoken above, then why do you believe you are encountering such a ghost?

You may say they are here for a reason, or for their reasons, and you would be only partially right. They are here for their reasons and for yours. Nothing happens without a reason and so therefore there is always a reason they appear to you.

Why do ghosts attack us?

Well I have never known a ghost to attack me per say and I have know many ghosts in my life. This can be a difficult to explain.

A ghost or ghosts do not have the ability to attack you unless you give them permission to. You have to give them permission to provoke an attack on your physical plain of existence. It is very difficult for a ghost one plain or vibration beneath our own to reach us other than to appear in a silhouette form.

We show fear, which is an emotion that is charged with energy and it opens a channel to the ghostly form. By doing this you give the ghostly form permission to channel back to you. When things can move around you, and noises can be heard, then marvelous materialisms can happen. All the time you gave permission for this to happen. The most frustrating part about all of this is most people including yourself may never realize that you're the one that gave this permission. It would certainly make my job a lot easier if you where taught this in high school or college as a prerequisite to a degree of any type.

, I don't give my permission to any type of spirit or soul without first reading there history through the Akashic records. Then after I have become aware of their path with me, then I give my permission for their presence to be. Now, for those less spiritual in presence at this point in time I would say that if you feel that you're being tormented by as unfriendly soul then call a professional that can reverse what has been set into motion by your presence or others.

How do we help ghosts?

Well in order to help ghosts you have to learn how to understand them, why they are here, and you need to make sure that they want you assistance. If you force your assistance upon them, you assume their Karma or worse you create Negative Karma for yourself.

A rule here on earth is we aren't allowed to force another to do something they don't want to. The same it true for ghosts.

If you force a ghost to do something it doesn't want, you will suffer the consequences through negative Karma which can follow you through life paths until the wrong-doing is corrected.

We help ghosts by living with them, respecting their spaces as they respect ours. The ghosts that I live with in my house are there for very specific reasons and I honor those reasons by leaving them alone to fulfill their life paths.

Now, if they wish to play with me or talk to me they are welcome to do so and thusly the same for me with them. They are beings just as we are beings they just look differently they we do. This by the way is called "Unconditional Love" for all beings.

When I see a pet that I shared this life with in a ghostly form I don't treat it any differently then when the pet was alive on this plain of existence. We continue to build on each other's experiences in a very positive manner. If you are experiencing a Ghost in your home, treat them with Unconditional Love and see what happens. If you see a positive change then you know that you were the cause of the negativity. If you don't see a positive change, call in a professional to assist you as you may not be the cause but just receiving the effects of others wrong doing.

Do ghosts suffer in a Purgatory State?

Well yes and no!

First, let's take the "Yes" part. If you are experiencing a ghost then they are living in a new state of life, one they may not remember and it can be very terrifying to experience. Think of it this way, you are suddenly pulled from one environment blind folded ,and then remove the blind fold and you realize no one can see you anymore. Wouldn't you get depressed for a bit until you found your ground or your comfort zone?

Most ghosts experience this type of atmosphere for the first part of their journey and it can last from a week to many, many years. It just depends on their individual soul and how much they chose to learn. This state that they are learning in can be referred to as a Purgatory State. Now, there are many different states of consciousness, so the side of "NO" is applied here. If a Soul requested to remain in the presence of the third dimension (one plane below the plane in which real people exist) then they will not live in a purgatory state because they exercise *the right to free will.*

With this "right to free will" they will then have the ability to see others like themselves in the vicinity or environment where they reside. They can then talk to each other take notes and do many activities together as a team. Hospitals are known for this type of environment or collective of ghosts working together to assist others to perfection.

Sending ghosts to the Hall of Records!

To understand the concept that a human being can send a ghost to the "Other side" may take some explaining and a lot of practice. The Hall of Records is a collective of records that are or were recorded on a soul's path to perfection.

Everything we do is recorded. Yes everything! And there is a place where these types of records are kept and it is called the Hall of Records. The Hall of Records is where we send all beings ready to move back into the Father bliss on the other side. This is a place where all souls go after working through a life path. They go to this place in order to learn more about their accomplishments from their experiences in any given life path. This is a place for our souls to recharge and to be fully accompanied by angels. The Hall of Records looks a lot like a very large library with angels everywhere to assist us in every manner. It is a peaceful place and warm. We see our loved ones, soul mates, and our kindred soul mates. We get to play and rejoice with all of them for as long as needed. See when we finish a life path we need to remember to return to our true spiritual selves and the Hall of Records helps us to do this.

The best way to send a ghost that is willing to move to the other side is to simply say it is time for you to go. If this doesn't work for you then call in a professional and make sure the professional doesn't just send them away or you could take on a lot of negative Karma. This type of professional should be a Reiki Master or a professional psychic of at least ten years of service in the professional realm. Take a good look around you and look at the professionals in their fields. It is to your best interest.

Just remember, once the ghost has been successfully moved to the Hall of Records you may not speak to them until your return yourself. If you wish to speak to this soul you will need to call upon a very special instructor. Call a Master Teacher. We are few and far between in this time and we channel the highest Vibrations allowed by Father God. We have the ability to speak to any soul on the other side and we can call in help unlike those on lower Vibrations. Now, this isn't to say that someone on a lower vibration can't do the work, because they can. However, they must go through many channels and require much needed assistance to reach the levels of that of a Master Teacher can reach in just thought alone.

For example, when I travel by a cemetery I simply say, "Anyone ready to go to the other side?", and if I hear, "Yes," well then I think through thought and send them in a blink of an eye. Many others would need to perform a ritual of sorts and pull in many spiritual guides to assist them.

It is important to remember that moving ghosts to the Hall of Records should be performed by the professional and the individual that wants a ghost to go or just simply say, "You're not needed here!"

Using White Candles for Protection

It is said that when you light a white candle the angels can see you better. In my heart this seems right because I can see them better too. I have used white candles in everything I do from meditation to channeling or just simply in my home office while writing this book. It is a comfort that I indulge myself in every day.

I always say you can never see enough of the purist souls, Angels. And to have the honor to work with them on many levels all the time is great indeed. White candles work well when you want ghost to leave you alone. A ghost has a hard time staying illuminated out of the shadows of darkness in our space and so you see silhouettes. When you light a white candle you then illuminate with the purest of flames and the ghost generally cannot compete with this level of energy and dissipate before your eyes.

The Angels can compete with this level of energy and come strolling in like a wave of fresh air. You will fill the room with so many of them they will comfort you and the ghosts alike.

Try it sometime and don't allow yourself to get spooked by the energies, there will be many of them and you will see only that of which you can handle at that time.

I would recommend placing the white candles around the house in glass containers for safety. Then sit in one of the rooms centered to the others and see if you feel any spiritual beings ghosts or Angels. You should feel light and airy, and start to fill with love from a source you may or may not recognize this would be an Angel or Angels in your presence. At first the feeling will be very minimal as they don't want you to become afraid of them. As you become comfortable, the Angels will feel your senses relax, then they will allow more Angels to fill the space and soon you will be giddy with happiness. Try it you won't be disappointed! If you have any problems call a professional.

NOTES

Resentment is like a glass of poison that a man drinks; then he sits down and waits for his enemy to die.

Nelson Mandela when asked why he was not resentful for his imprisonment.

Forgiveness

Forgiving Intuitively

We use many methods, but if you sit down and write out what it is that you are asking forgiveness for then you will have clarity. Our intent and how we say it, how we think it, and how we feel it makes all the differences in the outcomes.

The importance of the accuracy will determine your outcome, so the more positive your intentions the more positive your outcome. If you choose to ask for forgiveness then you are asking for Divine Intervention and know you are asking your spirit guides to open doors for the positive flow into your life. This takes work and time and as we all know most people are not into both at the same time. Now you have Divine Intervention rewriting the programs of many instead of one. Though in reality it takes a matter of seconds to do this work for spirit, it takes time to effect on our plane of existence. This time can take as much as a year to work out all that it affects and sometimes it can take a day. Let me give you an example.

I had the opportunity to sit in on a Felony trail against a young man accused of Sex Abuse in the first degree. The trial was set and the twelve jurors were chosen. The first day was based on documentation from the Prosecutor and the two witnesses.

The Defendant (accused) was sitting up front with his attorney and I could see many angels in the room. The defendant would cross himself every time he entered or departed the courtroom. I felt bad for him.

This man had no chance even in a court room in this type of case there is a 1 to 50 chance he would be found not guilty even if he really is not guilty. Our court system doesn't allow any room for errors as they rely on funding from the governments in order to provide the law enforcement that we currently have. It comes down to money.

Now, don't get me wrong. There are many professionals in the field that do wonderful and positive things, but they seem far and few between. There are many good ones, with the few bad being in powerful positions to dictate the will of the good.

This young man on trial was in an awful position because of the will of those whom thought power would overrule truth.

The young man called in Divine Intervention for three days straight and on the third day after all the deliberations and false accusations were proven wrong and without merit and by 3:00 p.m. a verdict was made. You're right he was found not guilty. The young man stood up and was so noticeably shaken by the experience. He thanked the judge and left with his party. The room was full of angels helping him and moving so many individual at one time that it took many in Divine Intervention to help all the people in ego to see the truths and set this one person free from the clutches of ego. This is but one example of how a Tools of Forgiveness can work through Divine Intervention.

 It is important to remember that when using your intuitiveness and forgiveness that you should always write what you want to do just so that you can keep it clear on your intentions. The clearer you are with your intentions, the better the end result.

Tool of forgiveness and how they work.

Let's see here, I should take a moment and outline the many different tools for you and then I will explain what they mean and how they work.

1) White Candles (again)
2) Calling on Angels for protection

3)Spirit Guides for help
4)Love (soul meaning deep unconditional love)
5)Peace
6)Learning experiences (their meanings)
7)Outcomes (Choices)

An example:

Let's say you're having a problem with a neighbor and you have had this problem for nearly ten years and the energy with them is absolutely volatile and now they are threatening to sue you for your involvement with your home and some clutter. The neighbor's anger level is now high and they have had it with your clutter. They aren't thinking about why you became a collector in the first place and they aren't caring to know. They just want it stopped and that is final.

Now, the truth is your clutter has made your home's value drop like a rock and so the same for the neighbor's homes and your home is also a fire hazard, which in turn is dangerous to the neighbor's home too. We all can learn from these mistakes, both the neighbor's and you, the cluttered homeowner.

1)We light white candles (in glass jars for protection from fire hazards) to invite positive pure energy all around us (we are setting the pace).

2) We call on Angels for protection (where everyone calls on angels so it is easier to associate with them). You simply say "Angels I give you permission to assist me now". Not hard to do.

3)We call in our "Spirit Guides" to assist us the same way we call in our angels.

4)We send "Unconditional Love" by way of thought to our neighbor's. So just think about sending "Unconditional Love" to each one of the offending neighbor's.

5)Bring into your thought the feeling of "Peace". Think of something that makes you peaceful like a warm soft sandy beach and a peach margarita or along those lines. As you think about this "Peaceful" place then apply that feeling to each one of your neighbor's.

6) Look at all the different learning experiences and write them down. This is a crucial part of the outline. You must look at the learning experiences and accept them. So for example, in this situation the learning experiences could be:

a) I collected too much stuff and it now is all over my property.
b) I'm a fire hazard for myself, family, and neighbor's.
c) My clutter is pulling the neighborhood's home values down.
d) My family is suffering from my collecting.
e) My family is suffering for my dilemma.
f) I'm forcing my family to suffer for my pain of losing a child to death.
g) I'm continually forcing my family to suffer while not taking the responsibility to recover from the death of my child.
h) Now, the neighbor's are sending me a message to stop, look, and learn from my mistakes.
i) The neighbor's don't know why I'm suffering in this manner.
j) They do not know why I'm forcing them to suffer in this manner.
k) I'm affecting so many people and their children and their pets as well as property.

7) Think of the *outcomes* (results) you wish to come from all of this experience. They should be along the lines as these:

a) I want to get better emotionally.
b) I want my family to stop suffering for my deeds.
c) I want my family to live the best life they can.
d) I love my children, both alive in this space and time, and those that have passed too.
e) I love my life and I'm grateful for my husband and my children to have the honor to be loved and to love back.
f) I'm grateful for my mother and my father to still be in my life.
g) I'm grateful to my neighbor's for helping me break this chain of events.
h) I'm grateful to my neighbor's for having the ability to voice what they are feeling in order to help me recover from my fears.
i) I want my neighbor's to recover too.
j) I want my home and the neighbor's home values to rise for the good of the neighborhood.

k) I want "Peace" with my children and I want to share their lives with them.
l) I love my grandson and hope that this experience only affects a positive manner to him.
m) I love myself!

Re-read from the first through the seventh list and then say thank you for assisting me. Now, you can blow out the candle and watch the end result. Should you need further assistance and you feel that what you did didn't work the way you wanted it to then call in a professional in the field. A Reiki Master is very good at healing all situations to remove a stressful situation with only thought, WOW! What a great idea, even though it took thought to create the situation in the first place!

Developing Intent to fortify you're level of forgiveness.

Developing intent to fortify your level of forgiveness is very easy to do. All you need to do is take any situation that you wish, such as the one in the previous sub-chapter, and intensify it. You now, just as you would add wood to a fire or more water to a glass, you simply add more emotion to the experience.

Most people only believe in what they can taste, feel, touch, see, smell and so forth. Let's break it down and make it really easy for you;

1. Taste - You can taste the nastiness of the flavor between you and your neighbor's and your family.
2. Feel - You can feel the stress building up and down drastically with your current children and husband and your neighbor's.
3. Touch - You can touch and move all your stuff from one place to another in a now exhausting and stressful manner.
4. See - You can see that you have no more room to add to your collection both inside the home or outside the home unless you expand the home more, which now costs lots of money for permits and builders.
5. Smell - You can smell the stress and the dying energies of life all around you as the energy for positive is slowly winding down to negative energy which really stinks and is ultimately stressful.

This whole time your intent was to secure yourself from the death of your child so you taught yourself to collect and never let go of material items to secure yourself from the pain of the loss of a child. In fact you have collected items that represent children in all manners. You have grounded yourself in this belief.

You can release this force of energy that has consumed you and your family and neighbor's. You can release it by using the intent level of unconditional love all for your child and you can place this *intent* in your life. You will release yourself from this destructive behavior and suddenly you will feel better, lighter, grounded, and peaceful.

We are creatures of habit and it takes us time to learn that we can heal ourselves with thought. You will need to repeat the process several times and each time you do you will emotionally feel less and you will remember much more positive memories that bring deep emotional smiles to your heart. The days will become eventful and enjoyable once again and you will have yourself to thank for the intent of the work that you did to forgive and heal!

Mantras and forgiveness and the powerful outcomes.

It isn't as simple as waving a magic wand to remove negative energies for deeper rooted and emotional issues that have taken years to create. This is the time for you to invest time, energy, and practice (ritual) in order to remove set ways and bad habits. There are many healing modalities out there, but none more effective than a Mantra.

A Mantra is the terms and conditions as well as the learning's for all parties involved and how you want the end result to ring true to you. It is sort of an agreement with yourself and the others involved without having to sign for it with all parties. You need to follow those directions carefully, after all this is about you and you would want to only take care of yourself with the best interest in mind.

This contract (Mantra) is very important. As you write the words and you speak them out loud, or to yourself, you are binding this contract with Father God and by doing so you are sealing it with your soul! This is why I describe it to you in detail. This isn't some elementary school fair where you're graded on it for points! This is your soul's quest through time.

This type of contract creates a demand for a change to the positive in your soul's records. The best and simplest way to explain this to you is to say you're agreeing to what you write down to the highest court of all. Whether you believe in Father God or any other deity known to human kind, it is still the highest of all contracts and not to be taken lightly.

Now that I have scared you to nearly death, I want to let you know something. If you make a mistake just simply state it in a Mantra and all is forgiven. We know that through the ages Mantras have been used mainly by the Hindu, Buddhist, and other Easter Cultures. Why? Because, it really works and not only works, but continues to work through all the ages and the Mantra's can be passed down through thousands of years while still holding the original and yet very strong meaning.

This is why I can't stress to you how important writing a Mantra is and how well it will work for you if you write it with "Pure Truth" in mind. Now, with this said let's talk about the degree's in which one may write a Mantra. These degrees have to do with how, why, what did you learn, and what sort of outcome you want to achieve. In addition to these degrees, you will need to learn how to voice your Mantra with emotion and a steady breath.

Degrees:

1) Basic – I would like to cool the jets of my flaming neighbors over where my BBQ sits.
2) Moderate – I want to help my children out of drugs and alcohol and into a better relationship with life.
3) Severe – You're in big trouble with a criminal/felony hanging in the not so distance future.
4) Catastrophic – You have lost your home to a fire, your car to flood, your family, your savings, your job, your life as you knew it to a Catastrophic Earth Changing Event in "your neck of the woods".
5) Death – You took someone's life by means of rape or you killed someone. Let us break this down for you to further understand how a Mantra would help you in each of the situations above.

Basic - A Mantra in this case would be written with the learning lessons of Where your BBQ site is offensive to the neighbors, maybe because of the smell or the smoke, maybe because of the ashes. Maybe they have a child's bedroom window near the smoke area and fear for that child's life. You would want to address the specifics by writing them down. Then you would think of how this has affected you such as the angry neighbors that have caused you stress and the fighting and arguing and write it down. Then you will think of how to help them maybe by moving the BBQ to another location or just by simple saying I would like to talk to you about this matter. Write it down! With pure Truth write down how you would like to see the positive outcome. Make sure that you cover all of these above in whatever order you see fit with the one exception of the outcome. This should always be last. Now, with feeling (emotion) speak the Mantra to life, repeat it several times and don't forget to light your white candle. I know it seems silly, but it really works. The rule of thumb is how many months have you suffered through this dilemma equals to how many times you need to read your Mantra. Once you're done, burn it by the White Candles fire. This seals the deal for you. (Remember to look for the signs of spirit speaking through others as you will receive an answer in a positive manner).

Moderate – A Mantra in this case will take just a little bit more work on your part. And remember, all you can do is you're best. It is up to the persons that you're fighting for to accept the positive energies you're sending their way. In this case you would write a Mantra starting with their incidents, list them all from the time you believed it started till current, don't be stingy here. It is very important that you list everything that has meaning to your request for Divine Intervention. Then list the learning lessons that you feel this individual is learning. This too is very important. (Remember, life is choc full of lessons and you cannot skip on them just because it is your family member.) Next, you need to write what your learning experiences have been and then of course what you would still like to learn, if anything. Take a deep breath down to your diaphragm and release slowly. You are ready to right the "Outcome". Make it completely positive, fair, pure, and truthful. This gives your Mantra driving force. Once you have written your Mantra you may speak the words; it is important to speak them clearly and with the emotions flowing, this gives the Mantra speed to your deity for immediate review and assistance to you and your family's needs.

Finally, make sure that your white candle is burning while you read your Mantra. You should read your Mantra out loud for as many times as your incidence and for as many times of your requests, in addition you should also read your Mantra for each year that you have suffered through this experience. Then once all is done, burn the Mantra and give this one at least two days before you start to see some changes. They will be little ones all around you, but you will start to see change, slow at first and then faster as the months move on.

Critical – This is a tuff one for the individual that is becoming or has become a criminal. Our justice system doesn't look favorably at anyone with a record and much less for the accused. So you have a pretty tuff act to follow here. Your Mantra has to be stronger than the justice system and you are the one that has to make that decision. You have to decide what you really want, what you really need and you must be pure and truthful as this will follow you through lifetimes and if you lie here you will suffer cruelly here. It is very important to be pure and truthful beyond a shadow of doubt just as the justice system tries to be. While writing this type of Mantra you have to be your own warden, your own prosecutor, your own judge and you cannot skimp just because you are in major trouble and want to hide or simple not deal with it. You have to come to terms with your mistakes and make them right. You have to come to terms with yourself and make yourself right. No easy task when you force yourself to admit that you where wrong for what you have done. Chances are whatever you may have done has proably been going on for many, many years and you will need to take time and really think about where all this started and don't leave out any details like family members, neighbors, friends, pets, or whatever started the trend. Look deeply within yourself.

The deeper you go the scarier it will be, but definitely well worth it. You literally, have to remove layers of time and habit forming experiences in order to get to the beginning and keep notes along the way so when you go to write your Mantra you will have the evidence that your case will need. Now, remember this too, you will not be showing this to any other human being. This is for your records only while you write your Mantra. With that pressure out of the way you can now start your Mantra. It is best that you work on the "subject matter" then move into all the people that have suffered through the ages because of your experiences and then write about how you have suffered too. Allow emotions to flow like, anger, frustrations, sadness, envy, disgust, sickness, whatever the negative energies are, you are to let them out like fear, fright, yell if you have to, but get it out of your system (mind).

A believer or not, I want you to call on your deities or angels for immediate assistance here. Allow, spirit to come to your aid! They're bigger than your-self and you will need every bit of help you can get and it will take a miracle of Divine Intervention to get you back on track in a "Pure and Truthful" manner, so don't skimp on whom to call for help.

Keep your thoughts positive. They hold weight especially in these types of environments and you will feel the presents of a pure and soft feeling like a cloud floating above you. You will not feel alone anymore as you write your Mantra as you purge your "True Thoughts" and feelings.

Once you have regained some strength from your emotions you can continue with your Mantra. This type of Mantra takes time to write, perhaps days or sometimes weeks. After all, you are a complex mechanism that wasn't devel-oped over night! And this is a complex writing for immediate assistance to your mental and physical being. You're requesting a change in your Akashic Records for the betterment of your life here on Earth and only you can re-quest such a change. Now, your spirit guides will also be doing requesting, though with your Mantra and this requesting is given a power unlike any-thing you have ever known on Earth. I'm not saying it is an end all or a do all, but you certainly will feel, see, and know of the positive changes all around you should you follow these instructions carefully and accurately!

Once you have written the body of your mantra now is the time to write your lessons. The more lessons you write (Lessons you have learned from this ex-perience) the stronger your Mantra will become.

After your lessons, you will want to write your outcome, what it is you wish. Try to write an outline of goals, Make sure you outline this in your Mantra. You will need to show your deity how you will pay back some time for your deeds and your special requests. This service should follow about a two to ten year plan. Not everyday, but a volunteer basis at least. Don't skimp as your deities won't skimp on helping you. Now, you're ready to take a one day break from writing your Mantra. Light a white candle and for those who are incarcerated either in a physical jail or a jail created out of their belief system. Imagine a pure white candle burning in front of you and then read your mantra out loud several times a day for at least a month or more. After, at least three months of reading your mantra before your white candle you can then burn the mantra. The smoke of a burning mantra takes it to the deity you have chosen. Also write on paper those things you want out of your life. Wet the torn pieces then flush it down the toilet, while you see it swirling away imagine it leaving you!

Catastrophic – When writing this type of mantra you are writing because of an event out of your control that affects you and loved ones. With these types of events you really want to write what you have learned and what you have suffered through and what you have to learn about it. Remember, everything happens for a reason and in these types of cases it is happening to a large group of people at one time. For instance, the Haiti Earthquake in 2009 affected so many beings and it was totally necessary for other people to step in and assist them. Sometimes these types of catastrophic events release steam building up from those without and it helps those that have to share through. As human beings, we need reminding to help those less fortunate than ourselves. Write a healing mantra for all those that have suffered and all the lessons that we have learned about this type of event. Then write how you would like to help, however small or large. Then write what type of outcome you would like to see ultimately happen. Once, you're done writing you can light as many pure white candles as you like. The more you have lit the stronger the message is carried. Don't forget to call on your deity or angels for assistance. It isn't just your angels or deity that you are calling on it is everyone else's too.

Read your mantra out loud with passion and compassion for all those that have or are suffering for a single cause. Once you have read it, place it aside. You will need to read this type of mantra at least three times before burning it. Let the candles burn down completely each time. This fortifies your unconditional love to those in need. After the third read, make sure that you have made your donation in some form and then burn the mantra. This gives it a powerful boost.

Death – This is the highest of all and it takes years to clear. This type of mantra is the toughest for us to get through. We as human beings have the hardest time forgiving those that have taken our child, mother, father, family members of any sort or our friends. It is the worst pain that one can ever experience, not just for the loss, but for the compassion of the one that took the lesser. I don't know about all of you that read this book, but for me my losses have been catastrophic. This type of mantra, allows for the two types of healing to take place. For instance, if you're the one that took the life, well then you would want to follow all the examples stated on the first four stages of mantra healing. Amplify how long you say this mantra, 4 to 6 months before burning it. There is one other piece that would need to be added to the mantra prior to the outcome. This piece must include empathy for your victim. You have to show how you're empathetic to the situation and then finish with the outcome. Now, should you be the person who lost the victim all you need to do is follow the first four stages and then show how your empathetic to the killer. Not an easy task, but necessary for your healing to take place, and for the healing of the person, the killer who took the vicitm out of this life path. As always make sure you're pure and truthful about your requests and answers.

It is important to remember how you speak the words in your mantra and what you are feeling in the process. Over time, you will lose the emotional baggage that follows these types of events. You will always remember the event itself, but the outlook and perception will have changed. Research shows that our memories change through the years. When you practice forgiveness, your memory changes from painful to a better understanding of the event. You should see positive results, but be careful not to expect results a certain way other than how you asked for it in the mantra. The results may come to you in many ways and it may take you a few minutes to realize this new result is in your best interest. And if the results are not what you're looking for simply write a new mantra.

Divine Intervention And The Power To Forgive

When we ask for divine intervention, miracles happen right before our eyes! Ants live in colonies cooperating because their survival depends on the cooperation. The cooperation is effective. You don't have just one soul helping you, you have millions! These souls come together to help rewrite your life path to your specification and they make sure it doesn't affect others around you. If it does then they rewrite their life path too. It is a monumental task, one that is completely mind boggling to our human mind.

Fortunately, for you, you don't have to think about such endeavors. You can literally focus on yourself or your loved ones around you. The complexities of this nature are enough for the human being's mind to handle. As a ascended Master Teacher, I have to always focus on the complexity of multiples of beings. Not just human, animal and/or insect, but dimensions too. It isn't easy, but it is well worth it!

A quote by Alexander Pope (1668) "To err is human, to forgive, divine"! This is so true. We came here to perfect our errors in our human form. However, you don't have to be, or relate to a divine manner in order to forgive. You simply find it in your heart (soul) to forgive others and yourself. Forgiveness starts by understanding we all have our perception and individual consciousness. Authentic forgiveness begins with giving up the state of consciousness that played out in the incident for an understanding of true identity as children of God.

We all forgive over time or do we? Most of us will for selfish reasons. To learn how to forgive divinely (authentically) you will need to learn how to forgive through selfless energies. That is, to let go of the ego for the greater good of all.

I met a younger man then myself recently. We'll call him Mr. G. Now, Mr. G is a nice man in his thirties and he is going through a rough time learning how to take care of his mother and still have fun being a younger single man. He wants to date and he wants to find someone to secure his life (selfish). Now, Mr. G has a good job and credit. He has been able to secure a good residence for himself and his mother.
When I'm around Mr. G he is always telling me how he hates to take care of his mother (his mother is heavily disabled) and he hates his job. When I mentioned to him it may be time to find a full-time caregiver, he says he can do it himself.
The truth is that he doesn't know how to assist her and he doesn't know how

to assist his own sanity in order to help successfully. I have helped him by teaching him how to look at others with selflessness. When I first met him he suffered from selfishness.

Today, he is packing up their old home and tomorrow he will be moving her and himself into their new apartment. This new apartment is nearly perfect for a disabled person. The rooms are wider the doors are much wider and the bathroom is designed for a person with disabilities. Initially he didn't want to deal with the truth around him so he didn't even look at all, for an apartment that would suit the needs of his mother. This is a part of the selfish movement in him.

 The other parts are his moods about not having what he wants and not having the security of an older person in his life. He is the oldest in his family and he has had to take care of his family for many years now. Some of us would agree that his time has come to be taken care of or at least free to take care of himself as he wishes to, but not at the expense of another!

Mr. G is learning now he can have it both ways as long as he understands for the good of all he will act out of selflessness. He is turning into a wonderful person to be around and he is enjoying himself more and more.
Here are some Divine examples;

Paramahansa Yogananda - a famous Yoga whom came to the Western Culture to teach Yoga and Meditation (a Hindu trait)
Gandhi – Master Healer and Hindu prophet
Jesus - Master Healer and Teacher
John the Baptist – Master Healer and Teacher
Saint Francis of Assisi – a Philosopher and a Prophet of God
Arch Angel Michael – Master Healer & Protector

All of these beings live still in their soul energy forms. And they are considered a few of the Divine beings that continue their works with us.

Forgiveness through divine intervention is one of the best ways for forgiving ourself. It is the hardest thing to learn, how to forgive ourself. This is the only healing that makes all healing work best. Authentic forgiveness comes when we can see that NO one could have acted differently at the time because of the consciousness. Each day our consciousness changes and unfolds according to what we know. This allows us to let go of the past and embrace our world in an aware way. Once we have achieved this within our own minds then the soul is free to take over and heal our ailment.

This is one the hardest tasks you will ever take on, but it is worth the struggle to achieve! You received this book to not only educate you, but to open yourself to the opportunities you will now notice and be able to actually handle. I bless you, and wish only the best for you, through divine intervention within YOU!

What happens when authentic forgiveness is truly accomplished through you?

You are then able to truly forgive others. Healing, just like everything else, is always a two way street. There are two sides to a story and in forgiving there usually are about fifty sides to a story. First, you accomplish the monumental task of forgiving yourself then you move on the next person, the one in your inner circle that you feel has trespassed against you and needs to be forgiven. You work outward from yourself to the farthest point needed to accomplish the healing.

You, The Next Messiah have the abilities just as a Saint or Angel has in healing, you just haven't fully awakened to the idea yet. You're reading this book which means you are on your way to awakening within you're soul-self.

Your self refers to the material that makes up the physical body. During your awakening process you are learning that your soul self and physical body, are two separate energies, one controlled by intelligence and one controlled by many forms of matter created by intelligence. Understanding that the physical body is real, but misunderstood by most of us, frees you. Science tells us we are the same energy as the computer and table and our atoms have more space inside than out. We may appear to be physical, but that is a trick of how our senses interpret all life. There is nothing solid. All life is based on intelligence and responds to intelligence. You have control of how and what you think. Your life is today what you have been thinking. Understanding this is a step toward forgiveness. You are freed from the world of the Pharaoh and Egypt (which represents physicality) to reside in the house of the Father, the land of milk and honey. Like the Prodigal Son the Father/creator source awaits for your return to your true destiny as a child of God

The Mind

We often think of single cells as lower life forms. The new biology has taught us that every cell, every molecule and atom are imbued with intelligence. You can think of a single cell as a small human. All life is made up of these cells, of these molecules that are intelligence expressing as intelligence, all connected by virtue of the invisible essence we call divine intelligence, soul. One soul, one intelligence manifesting in infinite variety as you, me, my kitty, my car your house, your garden. All of it is divine intelligence appearing in infinite variety.

There is intelligence in matter, not over or separated. You can think of intelligence as your soul. When asking for divine assistance you are not asking through yourself you're asking through our soul-self. You're asking through your intelligence-self. It is the awakened that seek divine intervention through themselves, through their soul-self the oneness of intelligence. Where do we go from here?

This is where you take all you have learned and apply it to your life. It is simple prior to learning something new to just say I want to learn it. If you really want to change, you will need a bible of sorts.

This book is a one of a series of three books which will give you the groundwork for you to grow successfully. Spirituality is like breathing. As you learn how to breathe, you learn how to control your breath to measure your environment. You do this with your spirituality.

Your spirituality moves with you in every environment, every type of job or career through everything. Further more, as we move into our new consciousness through human evolution we will need these types of education dialogues to carry us into our next chapter in humanity.

Don't be afraid to embrace the enviable as you chose to be present for this incredible experience to bring humanity to a spiritual level of understanding through unconditional love and peace.

Take back your powerful soul-self and apply that to your self as a human being. Allow your soul-self to embrace your day-to-day activities and watch as you open doors to your ability to create miracles. Yes, I did say you have the ability to create and manifest miracles. What humanity sees as a miracle is simply spiritual law and in the eye of the Father/God/Truth it is simply the way life was intended.

This is what I have been working on teaching you. Miracles come in all shapes and sizes. They come in people helping strangers for no other reason other than they heard the call for help.

I was outside my home one morning feeding our kitty, his name is Winner and my housemates pronounce his name as Whiner (as he meows a lot). I felt something wrong, lifted my head to notice a little Persian kitty stumbling in the middle of the road way. I walkied over to this little fellow and Winner followed me. The little kitty was so thin and sickly that immediately I knew that he needed food and water. Picking him up I saw the kitten had a very soft meow and a precious purr.

Taking him to the food bowl I placed him in front of it. Within seconds, the food was gone. I fed him another bowl of food and water. He finished it too and I named him Boo-Boo. I said, "Boo-boo came back later on and I will feed you again." He did. About four hours later I heard a little meow (different than Winner's) so I went outside and picked him up and performed Reiki on his body so he could successfully eat and absorb the food into his little frail body.

I used Reiki on his water and food too, then he sat down and Winner sat near him and he ate his food and relaxed nearby. Winner has set with Boo-boo ever since. My housemates have fallen in love with Boo-boo too. He is now nearly recovered from his ordeal and it has only been two weeks since he came for help. This in itself is a miracle for that soul being. The miracle was that I listened to my intuitive soul-self and heard his cry for unconditional love and peace.

This is true for every being, even the Earth! Everyone is calling out for help and it is now arriving in the forms of Master Teacher educators, Angels, Psychic's, alternative medical providers and much more. Take and heed the help, as you will defiantly need some form of it over the next ten years.

Living a Positive Life

Why is it important to live a positive life?

In layman's terms I would think it would be good to live positively so you can experience all things without pain or suffering. In a perfect world of unconditional love this would be what we are trying to achieve through our evolution. Intelligence is the purity of unconditional love so if we say that we are an intelligent species then we are saying that we offer complete unconditional love. We feel that we are invincible. In truth, we are as feeble as they come.

We are a fragile race that is dying every day and if not dying then we are killing ourselves off with war and poverty. Everywhere you look we are in a state of war with ourselves, our neighbors, our planet. What do we do when facing our own annihilation? We start to focus on living a positive life. We have to start at home, here ,where we can make a difference by leading an example of a people willing to create miracles for all to witness, by taking back our powerful soul-selves and applying our abilities to help our people in our own country. The importance of a positive life is not ego or material things it is unconditional love for a kitty, a neighbor, a friend, a family member that hasn't liked you for a long time and needs your help now, your fellow man and anyone else that needs your assistance including yourself!

The Next Messiah, YOU! Is really you. You have the abilities just as Jesus Christ shared while he was alive and through the Bible. He was one of the Ascended Masters who gave us ability to love unconditionally. To know that we can heal all the people, through the people, with the people, equals the soul-self working together in a team atmosphere through unconditional Love and intelligence. We find our miracles within our soul-selves when applying this intelligence to any situation. You develope a sense of teamwork and then that teamwork is applied to a particular environment and then a miracle is born as we see it in humanity.

Yes, Jesus was a Messiah too. However, he didn't end it there. The Next Messiah to be born is in all of us now as it was in every person or being that has come since. His messages and their views are carried through just about every master that lives or has lived through the ages. It is up to you to carry the messages of divine intelligence.

Living a Positive life is the beginning of a journey that most of us are terrified to travel. We have been taught to fear God. I ask why fear anything? Most of all God? The word fear traditionally meant to know. To fear God meant to know God. Do you have any proof God or anything else creates fear? We fear, or are afraid of what we know and/or don't know. Fear is a self-generated emotion. As we understand fear in the 21st century, fear is not the opposite of love but rather a lack of love in any one area. If you need to fear anything or anyone, fear your-ego-self! Healing and miracles can only happen through absolute love. Nothing is gained through fear.

I am a Master Intuitive Teacher descended and I have millions of years of experiences under my belt, but when I write, or do a reading, or teach I don't teach from someone else's point of view in their time I teach or read or whatever from my point of view in this time. What has been written is a history book or journal and should be treated changed beyond its original version. You lose the original energy of the artifacts original writings. You can review the original version in the Hall of Records and the meanings reside in our unconscious mind as archetypes. Today whatever you chose to write has your energies, your thoughts, You – The Next Messiah.

Living a positive life is embracing the changes of life, not fearing them!

Promoting A Positive Life Path

Promoting a positive life path isn't easy these days. You really have to focus on yourself and everyone seems to be focused on everyone else and what they did or didn't do and how they affected you personally or in business.

We each have a soul, a life path that we chose before entering into our physical experience. This life path of ours can have many different themes. You may have heard of some of the most popular ones like activator, psychic, rescuer, and catalyst. The reason behind the unlimited experience is so you can live a life many different ways and each time has a completely differ-ent physical experience. There are endless possibilities. The most important piece of information is that you are living in one of these endless possibili-ties. Your experience has been formed by your consciousness. This is a way I know works best to help you find your life path.

1) Contact a spiritual teacher such as a psychic, shaman, or astrology/nu-merology professional for a reading (this could cost between $50.00 dollars and $500.00 dollars depending on the professional and the years they have been training. The longer the better!).

2) Request a reading that defines your life path as you choose (the readings should take at least one hour to as many as five hours).

3) Seek out a good reputable Reiki Master that can help you to purge your life as you know it today. You need to align to your true life path (this can take many sessions and the more sessions you go to the better you will feel. I would recommend at least five or more sessions, if you do less you will suf-fer through the transformation with sickness, severe headaches, and nausea. Now this not to say that you won't have these types of symptoms you just won't suffer as badly.

4) Focus on asking your spiritual leaders like angels or fairies or other types of guides to assist you by giving them your permission to guide you in a positive manner in your life.

5) Be on the lookout for signs that give you the direction to follow. These are spiritual signs that we have talked about in prior chapters.

6) Relax and meditate along the way. You are not the only one going through this experience. I would recommend meditating at least 30 minutes per day, that is 15 minutes in the morning and 15 minutes just before you go to bed.

7) Leave time for private moments in your life for yourself and others. Don't forget that you are living in a physical world and having a physical experi-ence which means you need to experience in a physical manner whether you are engaging in a sexual act with your significant other or in a playful

act with your children. Get out and enjoy the life that you have going on around you. Go for walks randomly through parks and take small vacations and many as you can even if you have to drive. It is well worth it.

8) Live your life path.

Let me share something with you. I was a truck driver and a trainer for nearly twelve years. I never felt that I was on the right path. I was living the path my parents chose for me or guided me to live. You know, the one that you're supposed to grow up and go to college and eventually get married and have 2.5 children and be successful in your singular job for forty years (boring) then retire, hopefully with enough money to struggle with until you die! Now does that sound like most people's parents? Yes! Now does that sound like what happens today? No! Why do you think that is?

Well it is because people are changing, they are bored silly and they are bored sick. People want change for the better and instead most people suffer the worst because the change that takes place isn't good. Why not change for what is good.

Do you feel employers fired you for a reason of their own? No, and you would be right. They let you go because you needed to be redirected to your true life path and this is the only way to do so through your spirit guides and furthermore you were the one whom asked for it in the first place. The sad thing is you didn't realize you where asking for it.

Are you confused yet? Of, course you are. How can someone else affect your life when you chose it to happen? You attracted it through the Laws of Attraction. When you became bored with the job, you told the universe you just were not satisfied with yourself and the direction you are headed. Your spirit guides are on a mission to keep you on your life path, they have so much work to do. It is very difficult because you aren't listening to them nor are you looking for the signs they are allowed to send you. You then start to attract a new pattern to follow, this is the best time for your spirit guides to align you to your life path. This is the essence of living a positive life on your life path, change!

We all demand respect. Why? We demand it because we feel we have earned it and we believe as a people that we have earned it just by living day-to-day. Have we really earned the level of respect that we are demanding? No.

Respecting life is just as important as living a positive life path. Respecting life is understanding, the right to free will of others. You cannot go through life and not respect someone else's views without losing your self-respect. The right to free will means that each person has the right to free will through their choices. It is a spiritual law. When you try to control or limit another's choices you cause an immediate karma reflecting back to your consciousness of the situation. There is no stronger law in the universe than the right to free will and you have this right.

Respect comes from learning to live a positive life through respecting others. This is achieved when you fully understand how you affect negative energies upon the other by violating their right to free will.

How Does Karma Play With Your Life Path?

Think of it this way, you are in a really big "pin-ball" machine and you are the pin ball and every place that sets in the machine like a block or a bell is your life in every detail. You roll around and hit a bell, then you know you're on your life path because you gain points. However, every time you hit one of those blocks or circular dings you lose points or gain nothing. Worse yet, you are sent to another area of your life you just simply don't want anything to do with or it really gets ugly the more you ignore your guides.
Your goal is to earn more points through your game, right? You work at it. Now let's say that each block you roll into is negative Karma and you have to suffer through it. Then you will have to roll out of it in order to get to a bell for positive karma.

Once you are ejected out of the womb to start your descent down the path. sometimes you get really lucky and you move into a winner's circle and gain more points right. And with those points you learn more lessons in your life. And with each lesson comes a significant amount of good and bad karma. And how you roll with that karma with respect to the right to free will of others and how you roll in the game allows you to really do well or falter.

Ok, so maybe I have rolled myself out of your thoughts here. Let's look at this from the physical prospective.

You start life by being born to this world in this space and time. Once, you awaken to your physical body you start your life path as an infant. You start by tasting, feeling, listening, and seeing new things all around you. And as you continually grow you learn more and more. In fact, you never stop learning. The learning that you are doing is from these lessons. While you move through karma, this gives you a certain level of achievement. This level of achievement sets the goal for the next lesson. So Karma plays a great role in your life path as it is one of the prim factors in achieving your lessons.

It is important to say don't get overwhelmed with each lesson and even more important to say don't try to count how many lesson you will learn in a life-time. Remember, it is endless! You can learn as many or little as you wish.

The more you experience in the physical body the faster you grow in spirit whether you, like it or not. Because, you are a spiritual being, being human in a physical experience while on this planet, you are living through your own right to free will and you are experiencing all that you chose, both while you are here and prior to arrival.

Karma plays such an important role because it helps us to learn how to re-spect others right to free will. Every time you violate this right you bounce off into another direction off your life path and every time you respect an-other's right you bounce back to your life path. When I say respect another's rights I also mean your rights. See, you can disrespect yourself too. The ef-fects are the same.
While you're on the road to soul-self realization, you will need to keep in mind what karma (whether it is positive or negative) you do to yourself and what you may do to others while moving along your life path.

Keeping The Balance In Check

The best way to explain this to you is to say we have to learn how to balance everything such as our check book or food supply, how much food we give our pets or how much water we keep in our pools. We have developed a system of checks and balances in every aspect of our physical lives.

Forms of checks and balances are changing over time. The constants in the universe are flow and change. This changing is an affect of positive karma stepping in to balance the negative karma that has been experienced for the past 10 thousand years on earth.

These balances mean we will have to suffer through the changes of karma, both good and bad, in order to reset the earth's life path. Tough times are still to be had as breaking the chain of habits is not an easy task. Habits are the asleep ways of all beings when living in a physical life cycle. These habits set our day-to-day activities and can hinder our progression through our life path.

Breaking habits, takes time and focus, which of course slows our progress. Now our progress is so slow that we are being urged to pick up the pace and get moving again. This urge I speak of is the consciousness shift of 2012 and beyond. We are largely behind in the times of evolution! We are so far out of balance that it is taking a monumental adjustment in order to get us back on track.

These books that I write to you give you the ability to stay up on the times as the changing is now very fast. You will be able to follow a sort of bible if you will that reads like a manual of spiritual consciousness through the human experience in the very current life that we share as a people being human!

NOTES

Crystals grew inside rock like arithmetic flowers. They lengthened and spread, added plane to plane in an awed and perfect obedience to an absolute geometry that even stones - maybe only the stones - understood.

Annie Dillard

Sacred Stones

How can a Stone be a sacred tool?

Well easy, how old are you and how old is a Stone?

All through time, stones have been used for many types of tools such as, war, food, carving, decorating, roads and so forth. More importantly, stones are sacred tools and have been used in ancient times much as we use crystals today.

Many different types of stones are used in tombs, pyramids, temples, churches, buildings, monuments, healings, massage, art, and even creating balance in earthly energies.

Sacred stones are just like crystals except they are made from forms of compressed naturally occurring solid aggregate of minerals and/or mineraloids. The Earth's outer solid layer, known as the lithosphere, is made up of rock. There are three major types of rock they are igneous, sedimentary, and metamorphi

• 	Igneous rock is a form of crystalline cooled magma that once started out as very hot lava and then cooled and solidified. These are named according to their contents and crystal size

• 	Sedimentary rock is a joining of rocks and minerals over time generally by means of environmental changes such as water or wind over time to create stones like siltstone and limestone.

• 	Metamorphic rock is the transformation of an existing rock type from intense pressure and heat. This type of rock is sedimentary rock, igneous rock or even metamorphic rock. Some examples of metamorphic rocks are slate, marble, and quartz.

It is important to say that rocks/stones have been around since the beginning of the Earth. They are the oldest and first materials to be used in anything during humanities development and are found in everything that we have created and will create. If a volcano erupts and lava flows it will consume everything in its path for the duration of the route it travels. In short, what it consumes returns to a metamorphic rock in many years to come!

There was a time when humanity used the stone/rock as the main form of life in all ritual. .During this time (at least 12 thousand years ago) stones were made into sacred tools such as axe heads, polishing tools, chisels, bracelets and so on. It is important to say that all through the ages we have evolved to use rocks/stones in our diets, homes, rituals, and even in death. Even today, we still use the stones/rocks for our needs.

Can A Stone Really Be Used To Heal You ?

Today we have healing stones in massage, in meditation, and even stones in wisdom. These stones are in all countries such as, Mexico, England, Ireland, Scotland, India, and Iraq just to name a few.

The Mayan's of Mexico used charm-stone to heal and for its mystical and paranormal powers or energies. The Swedish island of Gotland and Ireland used a verity of bullauns for its healing abilities through healing waters. In England, Stonehenge is known as an ancient healing circle. There are so many of these types of healing antidotes throughout our world that it makes one sick as to why we have wars and are fighting amongst ourselves still and why we don't use them more often than not. These types of healing stones have been successful all over time and still we resort to chemicals to additions for the healing that we think we need.

Let us explore "Healing stones in Massage". massaging with water, heated or very cool river stones, have the ability to remain hot or warm for a long period of time due to the density of their metamorphic state. Stones, coated in oil, can be used by the therapist to deliver various massaging strokes. The hot stones used are commonly river stones, which over time have become extremely polished and smooth. You can enjoy the energy vortexes that accompany the stones as well as the deeply penetrated tissues relaxing under the heat of the stones.

There is another type of stone used, it is called the body-rock. This type of stone is used in applying and or amplifying the therapist's strength and focuses on the pressure points of certain areas. This body rock is a serpentine-shape tool and is carved out of stone. These types of stones are used even today in our spa and massage businesses.

The beneficial effects of massage include pain relief, reduced state anxiety and depression, and temporarily reduces blood pressure and heart rate. Theories behind what massage might do include blocking nociception (gate control theory), activating the parasympathetic nervous system, which may stimulate the release of endorphins and serotonin, preventing fibrosis or scar tissue, increasing the flow of lymph, and improving sleep.

• Pain relief: Relief from pain due to musculoskeletal injuries and other causes is cited as a major benefit of massage. In one study, cancer patients reported symptomatic relief of pain. Acupressure or pressure point massage may be more beneficial than classic Swedish massage in relieving back pain. However, a meta-study conducted by scientists at the University of Illinois at Urbana-Champaign failed to find a statistically significant reduction in pain immediately following treatment.
• State anxiety: Massage has been shown to reduce state anxiety, a transient measure of anxiety in a given situation.
• Blood pressure and heart rate: Massage has been shown to reduce blood pressure and heart rate as temporary effects.
• Attention: After massage, EEG patterns indicate enhanced performance and alertness on mathematical computations, with the effects perhaps being mediated by decreased stress hormones.
• Other: Massage also stimulates the immune system by increasing peripheral blood lymphocytes (PBLs). However, this immune system effect is only observed in aromatherapy massage, which includes sweet almond oil, lavender oil, cypress oil, and sweet marjoram oil. It is unclear whether this effect persists over the long term.

Additional dose effects help with:

• Pain relief; When combined with education and exercises, massage might help sub-acute, chronic, non-specific low back pain. Furthermore, massage has been shown to reduce pain experienced in the days of weeks after treatment.

•   Trait anxiety; Massage has been shown to reduce trait anxiety, a person's general susceptibility to anxiety.

• Depression; Massage has been shown to reduce subclinical depression.

• Dis-eases; Massage, involving stretching, has been shown to help with spastic diplegia resulting from Cerebral palsy in a small pilot study. The researchers warn that these results should "be viewed with caution until a double-blind controlled trial can be conducted". Massage has been used in an effort to improve symptoms, disease progression, and quality of life in HIV patients. However, this treatment is not scientifically supported, although in theory today most clinical studies have yet to support the age old adage of natural healings!

Stones in Meditations

Lecanomancy is a form of divination in which a diviner uses stones, oil and meditation, coupled with a basin of water, stones are dropped in the basin and the sound to the dropping along with the ripples formed are interpreted. When oil is used, the oil is poured into the water and the shapes it forms are interpreted. For meditation, the water is gazed upon, invoking a self-hypnotic state for divination.

Buddhism; Tibetan, Indian, Hindu, and East Asian esotericism there is the Mahamudra. It is the great seal or great symbol shown as a stone. It is a multivalent term of great importance in later Buddhism. The name refers to the way one who has realized Mahamudra (that is, one who has succeeded in the practices of Mahamudra) experiences reality: Mudra refers to the fact that each phenomenon appears vividly, and Maha refers to the fact that it is beyond concept, imagination, and projection.

Sri Lanka formed Monasteries, temples, and other various architectural forms all made from stone for the deities and dignitaries to worship as well as meditate in. These styles of buildings where varied over time and locations around the world similar styles where resurrected.

Forms of prayers are known to use Mantra's written into stones and then read continuously or consistently many times over in order to reach a deity or a level of deep meditation and peace. Muslims and Hindus use this form of meditation. These methods show a variety of understandings to prayer, which are led by underlying beliefs.

These beliefs may be that:

- the finite (people) can communicate with the infinite (deity)
- prayer is intended to inculcate certain attitudes or intentions in the one who prays, and can influence the recipient the one prayed for
- prayer is intended to train a person to focus (find peace) on the recipient through philosophy and intellectual contemplation
- prayer is intended to enable a person to gain a direct experience of the recipient
- prayer is intended to affect the very fabric of reality (illusion) as we perceive it
- prayer is a catalyst for change in oneself and/or one's circumstances, or likewise those of third party beneficiaries
- the recipient desires and appreciates prayer
- or any combination of the above

It is safe to say that through time and many forms of religions as well as beliefs that stones represent the greater symbols in which we find as a people to worship in. We as a people always look for something greater than ourselves to worship and stones have always been the mystical side or our lives.

Stones with Healing Wisdom

There are many great philosophers in today's world some are famous poets like Ray Buttigieg who wrote The Wisdom of Stones. Others are famous for creating fictional characters such as Dragon Valor, a video game, which depicts The Wisdom Stone stolen from a village. But, whether you are looking at a famous writer or a famous game, you will find that stones with healing wisdom are everywhere.

There are others such as The Book of Stones written by Robert Simmons & Naisha Ahsian which depicts stones as who they are and what they teach us? This is one of the books that I have learned many interesting points about stones and how to work with them in our illusionary world!

There are multiple books on the market these days that depict exactly what each stone is capable of doing for us and how we can learn from their knowledge and energies. I would recommend searching for the stone first then asking yourself to identify which book is appropriate. Your guides can work miracles here.

It is important to say that "Stones" are not limited to those of sand or metamorphism. There are many different types of stones and we will get into more of that shortly in the next book The Next Messiah YOU Part II.

Sacred Stones Of Our Ancestors

We have such a rich history with our ancestors and stones.You will learn that there is so much written and built upon with stones. It is simply amazing how much we take for granted in our space in time about 9,500 BC ago.

Every building in the Neolithic period was built out of stones. Stones where used at grave sites, in mausoleums, at the head of tombs, in churches, and in every religion. Homes were built out of stones. Here are a few examples of uses of Stones through the ages:

- Near Stonehenge in Europe is a site that shows signs of Mesolithic postholes that date back to 8000 BC
- Tumuli at Saint Michael built around 5000 BC
- Kercado built around 4600 BC
- Carnac Stones built around 4500 BC.
- Menec alignments built around 3300 BC
- Kerlescan alignments built around 3300 BC
- Kermario alignments built around 3300 BC
- Pyramid's built in and around 2500 BC

You get the point. The oldest of stone creations built by beings, whether by human or otherwise, dates back to about 12,500 BC. Let us explore a little bit more detail about each of these ancient stone creations and their uses through the eras;

Stonehenge in Europe was a place of burial from its beginning to its zenith. The cremation burial dating to Stonehenge's Sarsen stones place it from this later period that perhaps extends to nearly 6500 BC. The outer stones show the Mesolithic postholes dates back to nearly 8000 BC, though most believe that they were not filled with stones, but with wood and may have never fully been used at that time. Stonehenge's construction started in and around 8000 BC and continued to about 1600 BC. Quite a long time for construction. The construction continued in five phases over 6400 years!

Today, we still know so little about Stonehenge as there are no written records on the extremely old monument. However, what remains of the monument are still heavily visited by those interested in healing and meditating,. There are even rituals that still take place at this historic site. These rituals are performed by religious groups and spiritual groups. There is still debate on what type of stones it took to create the monument, some say it is iconic stone others say it is made out of bluestones. The energies locked into all the stones at Stonehenge is what drives the mysteries of healing powers and sacrifice. We as human beings are always drawn to the mysteries of our cultures.

Tumuli at Saint-Michael are several mounds of earth built over gravesites around the world, most are called Tumuli's. Most show a passage leading to a chamber, which once held a Neolithic artifact's. Saint-Michael is one of the more famous locations for these types of Neolithic artifacts. Saint-Michael was constructed in two time-periods the first was in 5000 BC and the second in 3400 BC. Though today the building looks more like a mound of earth it really is built out of stone in a pyramid design. The chapel there was built in 1663 AD, and today there is a re-creation of the original chapel. The tomb, with its original stone casket, was discovered in 1900 and again in 1907. This Tumuli at Saint-Michael is a religious tomb site for the dead to be remembered and rest in peace.

Kercado is a rare dolmen (a dolmen is a considered to be a tomb) still covered by its original cairn (a cairn is a human-made pile of stones). It is located south of the Kermario alignments and has a small menhirs (is a monolith that can sit on top of a tomb chamber or burial site as well as alone) on top. Previously surrounded by a circle of small menhirs, the main passage leads to a large chamber where numerous artifacts were found, including axes, pearls, arrowheads and pottery. The Kercado was constructed around 4600 BC and it was used for nearly 3000 years.

The Carnac Stones; where constructed nearly 4500 BC and support nearly 3,000 prehistoric standing stones. They were erected by the pre-Celtic people of Brittany, and are the largest collection of megalithic stones in the world, consisting of alignments, dolmens, tumuli, and single menhirs. The local people say that the stones in Carnac represent a row of soldiers that were turned to stone by either Merlin or Saint Cornelius. Either way the stones stand in perfect alignment multiple rows, a very powerful site to witness. The Carnac Stones where created in a series of stone formations called Menec, Kermario, and Kerlescan alignments.

The Menec Alignment was formed with eleven converging rows of menhirs stretching for nearly 3,822 ft. There is what remains' to be stone circles at either end.

The Kerlescan Alignment; was formed with a smaller group of 555 stones further to the east of the other two sites. It is composed of 13 lines with a total length of about 2,600 ft. At the extreme west, where the stones are tallest, there is a stone circle, which has 39 stones.

The Kermario Alignment; was formed with in a fan-like layout. It consists of 1029 stones in ten columns about 4,300 BC and a stone circle is at the east end.

As you can see we do have sites known to be very spiritual and religious in nature but we are not limited to just these. We also have many other pyramids, tombs, and monuments to boot. Here we name just a few:

• Pyramid of Khafra (known today as the Pyramid of Giza)
• Other ancient pyramids of Egypt
• Nubian Pyramids at Meroe
• Tombs and sarcophagi from Hierapolis
• Tombs of Pe're Lachaise
• Megalithic Tombs
• The Parthenon from Ancient Greece
• The Taj Mahal in India
• The Cristo-Rei in Almada, Portugal
All are made and ritualized from and around stones!

Stones And Their Consciousness

What you don't believe is that stones can have their own consciousness. At the very least stones can act as amplifiers for our consciousness. For instance, say you want that new car. (Ok, don't laugh at me, but with me.) You would take a stone that you're familiar with, say a nice piece of limestone or sandstone (you can even use marble if you chose) and then you place it between both hands, like your praying with it. You focus with all your might and think of the car you want. By doing this, you are impregnating the stone with a memory and you will tell the stone how you will get it. The stone will remind you to remain on your path. You may feel frustrated with your end-results. However, you will remember that you didn't follow your original plan and the stone will not wave a magic wand for you! Nonetheless I would like to take you on a journey briefly of a couple of stones you may want to consider working with first. They are adamite, amber and angel aura quartz.

Three very different and very powerful stones.

1) *Adamite* works with the Solar Plexus and the Heart Chakras. It has the ability (already pre-programmed into its consciousness) to effect positive flows in joy, love, creativity, enthusiasm, and perseverance. Adamite reflects the elements of Fire and Wind. It is said that when you hold Adamite in your hands you can feel lighter and clearer. Adamite will help you to align your heart and solar plexus chakras when used appropriately.

2) *Amber* works with the solar plexus chakras. This is for balance. Finite amber can be as old as nearly 60 million years. Amber has the ability to work with light, warmth, solar energies, clarification and healing. When used appropriately, amber can become your best friend while working with spirituality. Amber reflects an element of earth and balance.

3) *Angel Aura Quartz* supports the crown chakra as well as higher functions of thought and intent. When focused, one can uses this type of quartz for uplifting, peace, serenity, and expanded awareness. The essence is Wind. It is best to sit with this quartz and meditate at first, then you will slowly learn how to achieve an alighnment with this very specific type of stone.

These three types of stones are for a beginner's level. You should learn how to work with them, each as individuals and altogether as a team.

The solar plexus of your body represents the main intelligence source as a part of your soul. When your soul is balanced you can obtain clarity in your works whatever that maybe.

The next location that I described to you has to do with your heart. Your heart is the main function of your physical body and needs to be in balance too.

Your crown chakra is your physical mind and etheric is your spiritual mind. These two points of interest must be combined into one in order to become spiritual aligned. This alignment facilitates awakening.

During the awakening periods of the physical body, your spiritual body is working on merging into your physical body thus creating a whole being. By using various levels of consciousness, we awaken various levels of our being and growth is facilitated. By using stones to support this process, we achieve success.

Stones And Energy Fields

Unseen by the human eye are a series of energy fields that make up every being on the planet including the planet itself. Energy fields arise from energy auras that each being generate even from birth to the end of their manifestation.

It is indeed true we do create an electrical charge and so does every living from the trees, plants, and the planet. We are mini powerplants of energy. Each form vibrates at a different vibration. If we matched each other's vibration, we would be able to blend into each other's bodies.

Stones also vibrate with their own rate and level of vibration. These stones have their own energy fields. I'm a very high level vibration and I communicate with the highest level beings because my vibration is similar to their vibrations. I work with many stones, crystals and these crystals that work with me vibrate on a very high vibration. Not all crystals vibrate on high vibrations and it is vitally important that when searching for a stones of any kind that you feel the energy of each in order to establish the right stone.

When I was first learned about stones my master guide Kastian mentioned I should speak to a specialist in the field. So I went to a company in the Northwest territory called Crystal Awakenings located in Vancouver, WA. They were overwhelmed by my energy and even mentioned that my own vibration made them feel high! They were very knowledgeable and the books and a series of crystals I purchased from them have really enhanced my abilities to formulate to a finite detail.

Don't limit yourself potential due to fear you may make a fool out of yourself. Humility strengthens the soul and the personality. Understanding helps create your spiritual connections. Your research and your studies are the foundation that you build your life on. Following this business plan of sorts gives you the ability to follow your life plan as you had once written prior to your awakening in the human body.

There are many, many levels to vibration and maybe I will be asked to write about those levels in another book. For this book, however, we will follow a simple three level understanding. These three primary levels of vibration can inhabit over a thousand vibrations levels per singular level. For example:
Level One Dull – This would be the vibration of humanity
Level Two Chiseled – This is the vibration of insects and animals
Level Three Infinite – This is the vibration of spirit

Level One Dull - I place humanity at the bottom because most of us are not awakened yet! Also, the vibrations tend to be very low or slow.
Level Two Chiseled - is of animals and the reason for this is because animals are intuitively inclined based on instinct.
Level Three Infinite - Spirit has a much higher vibration and even in Spirit there are millions of vibration levels. But, for the time being let us kept it simple!

The Stones Energy Fields of vibration

Each stone has its own energy field a vibration that resonates (it is their aura's) and here are some examples:

• Jet – a black or dark brown variety of coal. Its energy field is smoky grey and vibration is infinite for purification and protection.

• Kunzite – is the pink-to-violet form of spodumene, a lithium aluminum silicate. Its energy field is light rose and varies in intensity of color. The vibration is chiseled for divine love, emotional healing and activation of the heart's knowing.

• Larimar – Larimar is a form of blue pectolite, a sodium calcium silicate mineral. Its energy field is the color of bluish-green water. Its vibration is dull for calming, soothing, cooling the emotional and physical body.

You will find that any dealer you work with in these types of stones will describe them in many different forms, each appropriate to their status, and their own vibration abilities. It is important to understand each of us resonates a very specific vibration and at that particular vibration is where we learn. And as we grow, we expand to higher vibrations, thusly gaining a higher perspective of life.

Creating Balance With Stones

We have discussed stones as sacred tools, healing modalities, consciousness of stones, and energy fields. None of these make much sense if you don't have balance! We need to understand and use all of what we learn to acquire balance. If you dive into purchasing four to ten different types of stones and then you decide that you want to achieve resonance with the stones, you will become overwhelmed. It is best to start with one or two different types of stones to get accustomed to them and let them get accustomed to you. Remember, they are beings too, just vibrating at a different rate than you.

While learning to understand your new stones, it is also important that you learn to work with them, each on their own level of course. The amount of energy you place into working with each of your newly found friends will be mirrored back to you. This is why it is important, if not imperative, that you start simply.

Learn every detail about each stone. For instance, diopside is a calcium magnesium silicate. If you're one of the few people that are allergic to magnesium silicate then I wouldn't recommend working with this stone. However, if you can work with magnesium silicate then this is a very good stone indeed. This stone works with connecting with the Earth, opening of the heart, healing, balance, and subtle perception. In every stone, there is an element and this stones element is earth. This stones chakras are heart, root (for grounding), and earthstar (below the feet). You too can learn all of this information.

There is much more to share, however, that is in another book. You may want to take notes from the professionals in the fields of stones. Through their experience they have learned and will guide you in your journey with stones.

Take your time and let the stones resonate with you in your palm of your hand. You will feel and small vibration or shimmer through your hand as you embrace this very unique being. When this happens from time to time you will feel a joyful feeling in your heart unlike anything you have every experienced in your life.

You will know soon enough as to which pieces of stones resonate with your vibration and those that do not. Those that do not, you won't feel anything. And those that do, you will feel a lot of new vibrations that will inspire your heart to learn more about them.

It is said, that each and every one of us will find many kindred souls along our journey on this earthly plane and they come in many forms. Stones are one of those forms. Let your stones balance and resonate with you so you can grow and expand too.

Our intention creates our reality.

Wayne Dyer

Intention

What Is Intention?

Intent is the purpose upon which we act. The soul is considered the purest of intelligence and therefore has the clearest of intent. The ego sees its own intent based on beliefs (which may be very wrong, lack fact or just self serving). However the cosmic intent, the intent of the soul to return to the creator source always remains.

The subconscious mind – holds all the information we have gathered, our lessons, as well as what we think. Pure energy enters into the senses and is identified according to the experience. Our intellect then formulates an assumption upon this subconscious information (emotions and experiences). This assumption becomes a belief upon which further action and decisions are based.

The Spiritual Mind or Soul/Intelligence Mind – see's only truth and so perceives only truth and it is not based on beliefs and assumption. The spiritual mind bases its insight on spiritual law and axiomatic thought. This thinking is straight thinking in the abstract and is not tainted by the ego will. Spiritual thinking is based on Truth and that which is so about the nature of reality.

Our cosmic intent, the spiritual intent of our soul, is to remember the Truth of our self, to remember who and what we really are, children of God/Creator/Truth. In this remembering all the secrets of the universe are revealed to us.

God/Truth is all there is. This includes our senses, apparent physical body, ego, everything that appears in our consciousness. Truth is that which is so, that which is not so is not Truth, therefore Truth is all there is.

Intent is by all means the very driver in the vehicle of manifesting anything in our lives, but if you have never been taught how it works well then how do you figure your intending to do something right or intending on receiving something you requested right. Have you ever noticed that what you requested and what your received tend to be different?

1) it takes some education on the subject of intent in order to figure it out.
2) it takes practice since we are creatures of habit!
3) it takes patience, something that most of us have to learn before achieving.
4) it takes time.

When requesting something to come to you like a new car or a home or a family member to call; it takes time to manifest because our level of intent changes throughout the thought process.

For example: Let's say you would like to contact a long lost friend and you have warm wishes for this friend. Do you think your intent will be strong or weak? In this case your intent would be strong and the friend would call you nearly immediately. Try it and write it down or make a metal note of it. Then when the friend sees you or calls you write it down again and see how long it took for them to hear you're intent spiritually! You will be amazed on how fast this system works when you are focused and show high signs of positive emotion through the physical mind coupled by unconditional love of the friend through your spiritual thoughts.

Why do I need to learn about intent?

You need to learn about it because in order to manifest anything you must have clear intentions.

Wow, it is so important to make sure you get it right the first time so when you achieve your end results you will be closer to your example of the original *intent*.

Think about it, would you leave and drive your car without fuel?
Would you live longer than a month without food?

Wouldn't you freeze to death without heat?

Intent is just that to manifestation. One cannot survive without the other through our physical body and mind. We are a fragile race of human beings and thusly we vibrate on such a level that allows us to use our physical minds verses the brawn of our bodies!

Intent is the purest of thought. Now if you where to use intent in a negative manner, well then, your thoughts would still be pure but would not conclude with positive energy. Thusly, I wouldn't use this information for a negative result as this negativity will backlash you and leave you with suffering immediate negative karma. However, when using Intent for a positive result you will create positive karma. It is really that simplye The Universal Consciousness doesn't make this hard to understand it only simplifies. It is mankind or human kind that creates such an illusion of negative results.

For instance, in my house I have three housemates and they watch the news every night and they always complain about the news always showing negative results. This would be mankind's best results! Why not show how a neighbor or neighborhood rallies together and helped the one family survive personal tragedy!

Have you ever wondered why at Christmas time of year everyone is happy because for once in the year they are not fighting through the negative illusion placed upon the masses by those whom intended to control? At, Christmas time the positive outweighs the negative and suddenly you can see all around us the positive that happens everyday! We think it only happens during the Christmas time of year, but it doesn't. It continues all the time.

See it is our illusions and illusionary training through the ego physical mind from early childhood to college level and even higher when you leave out the spiritual mind/intelligence soul mind. (One doesn't not exist well without the other.)

So, in thinking about it you have only received half of your training in this life time. You learned about humankind, but didn't get the training you needed of the spiritual kind. These books that I write gives you the training of a spiritual kind in a very basic form. None the less, the facts are the facts.

You cannot survive with only half the truth to live by. In today's world those that survive well are those that understand the spiritual "Laws of Attraction" and intent is one of the most powerful rules in this spiritual law.

It is vital that you learn these rules in order to follow the manifestations or dreams in your life that you wish for yourself and family as well as your neighbors and they must be of a positive and pure thoughts so that the end result remains the same, positive and pure.

Using intent in a negative manner will always find you with negative karma within this life time. Now that you can see why it is so important for you learn about intent, and the following sub-chapters will outline for you the many levels of intent and how to work with it in your daily lives.

How Can Levels of Intent effect a positive change in my life?

Well let's look at this in two levels, first is "Levels of Intent" and second is "Positive Change".

First, Levels of Intent are;

- Emotion
- Integrity
- Subject
- Expansion

Let us take look at the first Level of Emotion. As we have all experienced emotion is a powerful measure in our lives. Think about it. When you say to your significant other "I love you" does it not have a major impact on that persons life? Of course it does. So why not work with Emotion as a power-ful tool with Intent. I mentioned about the "Laws of Attraction" right and in those spiritual laws Emotion is used to control your thoughts for a positive or negative result.

For example: you want to have a friend call you, then you think in your mind with emotion how wonderful that friend is and you sit on that thought for a few minutes and then you move onto another thought. A day later or so that very friend calls you and you are surprised because you never thought in your physical mind that they would hear you. However, in your spiritual mind they did!

This is a prime example of working with your spiritual mind and it taking effect immediately and then triggering synchronistically a chain of events to unfold. In this case, your friend giving you a call. This happens more often than not and most of us take this to be a coincidence and in your physical mind that would be true to your human development. However, in our spiritual mind, there is no such thing as coincidence, There is only synchronicity, truth. Your emotions of feeling really good memories of this friend sped up the process for that individual to call you.

However, we as human beings always make things out to be much more difficult, so if you try this and nothing happen, well try again until it does. Each time you try, you change your behavior and eventually success wins the day. You must remember to place your emotions appropriately, in other words think first what you really want, then feel the emotion for that subject whatever it maybe. This gives you the chemistry in order to summons the subject you desire in a positive manner.

The second "Level of Integrity" is a concept of consistency of actions, values, methods, measures, principles, expectations, and outcomes. Integrity is regarded as the quality of having an intuitive sense of honesty and truthfulness in regard to the motivations for one's actions. The truth is that if you don't have this type of integrity then your requests will go on unnoticed in manifestation or they may take a much longer time than initially thought.

When coupling Integrity with Emotions you really power up your manifestation abilities. But, that isn't all of it. It is also very important that you live by this understanding and apply this understanding in regard to all relationships.

I can't stress enough to you the greater importance of this Level! Let me give you an example:

Let's say you are running for a Presidency and you promise so many endeavors and your constituents vote you into power and then you don't follow through, what happens? You won't survive the day. You will be impeached, or murdered, or worse. You won't have any work once your terms is completed, why? Because you're Integrity was not in truth!

Remember the definition above states that you must be honest and have values with your actions. The above example happens all too often in this day and age. We have some wonderful Politian's out there and they get swept up into the propaganda of press and political woos! Unfortunately they lose the very values that once placed them at the top of their game.

Let us look at another example:

Say you're an at home mom and you have four kids and a husband that is never home because he has to work all the time to make just enough money for shelter and food on the table. You are frustrated because you don't have the help that you need at home and your husband is frustrated because he doesn't get to spend time enjoying your space and the kids.

Now, both of you wanted children, but neither of you wanted the massive responsibility of maintaining them singularly. In the beginning, one or two children where planed and you both felt wonderful about it. This planning was built on Integrity. However, as you grow, the job changed and more children arrived, your integrity changed and now you're over whelmed with abundance! Now, you begin to fight with each other and soon you're in divorce court all because you became greedy for more! Think about.

The point is when you are working with emotion and with integrity you also need to exercise patience and limitation. Set the pace but don't buy the farm and manage it yourself. You will lose. Abundance is very good when you can manage it. But, when you become overwhelmed with abundance you have to stop asking for more.

In the case above, once you leveled off with two children the safest understanding would be to take a break and see where it goes for about a year or so.
Another example of *integrity* is the use of power. Think about power and what this means to you? What is power? How do we posses it? Really, power is just a verb to describe what you really are talking about isn't it! Power, is none other than a manner to explore control within the ego principle known as mankind!

Mankind describes what? A human being! Or a being! See a human being is just that. Not defined by male or female. Humankind or human being is described by being human not mankind.

Now, take power created by mankind and apply being human to it and what is the outcome? The outcome is a powerful spirit experiencing being human in a physical body of either male or female or both!

Now, that I have your curiosity in check let's look at "Power", Power is none other than a rate in which we measure energy through the spirit. In short, if you are said to be powerful, well then, you have a lot of energy that passes through your bodies both spiritual and physical. That's all.

Spirit doesn't measure power the same way being human does. In the spiritual world we measure vibrations by means of levels and they are not measured up or down, but expand outward from the soul.

If you still find the need to state that a Descended Master Teacher is a very powerful being, then you must apply the correct definition to the subject. A Descended Master Teacher vibrates at high vibrations and therefore moves a great deal of energies through all vibrations back to the soul. So indeed if you're a being that vibrates at a higher vibration, well then, you can move more energy thusly, and in the ego principle be considered a very powerful person.

Now, with this long version spelled out let us look at "Integrity" from a powerful space. As mentioned above integrity is a form of, but not limited to a concept of consistency of actions, values, methods, measures, principles, expectations, and outcomes. In short you don't have to be a powerful person in order to apply "Integrity". You do need to be a being with sold values in order to apply "Integrity" with honesty and truthfulness.

See it isn't that important to get the order right however, it is important to get the values right the first time otherwise you will be trying many times in order to attract what it is your going for.

With the new conscious shift that is concluding very soon, you will need to have this type of information to learn from in order to understand the evolution of being human.

Integrity is all these things as more. You must look within yourself to find your *integrity*. The best way to do this is to sit down in a warm comfortable space and follow these instructions:

1) Get really comfortable.

2) Sit in a quiet space in your home or outside wherever you are most at peace and quiet. That means no noise other than maybe birds and light wind.

3) Make sure that you have a piece of paper and pen or pencil to make notes with.

4) Now, close your eyes (this helps to remove distractions).

5) Start to think about whom you are and then ask yourself this question, "Where does my integrity lay? Am I a being of integrity? How do I apply my Integrity best?"

6) Now, the first answer that comes to mind *write it down*. Don't delay, don't think about it, don't stop and say wow. Don't do anything of the sort. Your ego principle trained mind will make this very difficult for you to understand because you were taught in the physical body to not believe in any of this since you were born. Now, you must take control and remove this training since it no longer applies to this day and age.

7) You many need to work on this part for awhile don't become discouraged if it doesn't work the first time.We are a creatures of habit and it can take a while to break old habits and ways of thiinking. It may take a few tries to hear the answers you're looking for. Remember to be truthful and honest and don't cheat yourself into believing a lie.

8) Now you will take this information and review it thoroughly, you must feel the emotion that comes from each of your written notes. It is similar to those that act on the big screen. They must feel the emotion in order to really *nail the part* as it where. The only difference for you is you cannot lie about this as spirit will not recognize you and they will move onto the next person to work on their request first. Furthermore, should you lie to yourself you are in fact lying to spirit since you are a spiritual being, this will only bring heart-ship to you instead of a positive result to your new founded actions you will suffer a negative result. We call this instant karma and you will feel it within hours of your decision.

9) Now that you have figured out what it is that defines integrity, you are ready for the next step. Please remember that integrity is pure positive thought with no harm to others and for the highest good of all!

10) Now we can move on to "Level three your Subject"!

The third level is *Level of Subject* this may be one of the most important levels in which you will identify easily with. See it isn't just simply enough to choose what it is that you're interested in, but importantly what it is that will help you with your day-to-day expansion within this new consciousness.

The values and energies we placed in the physical world are quickly losing ground energetically now. As we evolve to being more spiritual in nature, we also will evolve as a species. This evolutionary process has taken hundreds of thousands of years to evolve to what we are today with one little exception. We have evolved very slowly because we left out spirit and only tried to handle the situation through the ego. We no longer need to do things in the same way. Humanity is beginning to awaken to spirit without dying to do it. This is unprecedented and only spirit could pull this off. This is why those of us who are able to channel or write can deliver the messages as a precursor to this evolutionary process. This is where you, the reader, are very lucky that you don't have to endure the endless hours that we have to in order to deliver the messages sent by spirit to you!

Level of Subject is in fact the very reason you have picked up this book to read it. You were guided to this book for an educational purpose in order to evolve within your own spirituality. Now, you may choose any subject you would like and you may choose through *integrity* how you wish to experience this subject.

So let's say for example:

You would like to see your parents that you have been estranged from for a very long time. You would first sit down and write out your emotions. Then you would write out your integrity. Then you follow through with your subject and furthermore you would follow with energy expansion of which we will get into next.

Now, you haven't talked to them because of a serious misunderstanding that took place nearly two decades ago.. Please take a bit of time and be thorough and describe how you feel about this matter. Once completed, set that information aside.

Now, pull out a new piece of paper and take a really deep breath and inhale down to your diaphragm and release very slowly. Now let us work on how you want your emotions to play out with the completion of this Intent. Make sure that you don't cut corners just because! It is better to be as honest with yourself as in prayer to God or any other deity. Furthermore, it is important for you to describe a positive outcome for your emotions only. Pause for a moment and complete your *emotional* dialogue. This should take about fifteen minutes.

Now, let us review the subject with new circumstances. You would like to be in good form with your family (parents). And you would like to spend several special holidays with your family once again. This would be your new subject.

See it isn't that hard. In fact, the hardest part about working with Intent is learning how to get through the original emotions that lead you down this path to begin with. Once you have that figured out you can do anything. Just like actors in a movie, you will be able to review your own dialogue and then fully with integrity act it out in your life

Ok, we are making really good time here. Let us move on to the next Level.

The forth level is called *Level of Energy Expansion.* This may be your most difficult level in the beginning and then it will become the easiest level during your ventures.
Energy Expansion is controlled by your emotions and integrity. The velocity of this expansion will be determined by how strong your emotions are and how clear your intensions are through integrity. In short, if you are willing to really review your integrity and get it down pat then you can really get the speed accelerating within the energy expansion.
The emotional part is simply that it is being delivered to your family in this case. The energy expansion is that which is carrying your emotions and it will get through by spiritual means of communication through the soul rather than the intellect.

When working within spirit you are accessing the very essence of you. You are not just a random physical body that goes through life blindly. No, but rather a being of light and goodness that now has the ability and means by the masses to really communicate through consciousness.

Have you ever heard of *Ant Consciousness?* Ant consciousness means working with patience. It also means working together as a team through consciousness. Do you feel that you don't have consciousness? Well I'm here to tell you every person shares a very powerful consciousness. We call it being human!

In short, as a human being we all are connected to each other whether we recognize this fact or not. And with this type of connection we have the ability to create and to Intent our outcomes as we wish them to be as long as they are with the character of integrity.

Now, that you have learned what is necessary in order to work with Intent let's bring it all together now.

1) First you must write down your feelings (emotion) on the subject prior to creating your outcome. Then you must write down your feelings that you would like to experience at the outcome. Remember to make sure that your outcome feelings are for the highest good of all and with no harm to all.

2) Second you must write down your integrity, how you want this to work out and what do you want from the integrity point of view. For example: would you like your family to love you unconditionally and maybe you could love them unconditionally too?

3) Third, you must stipulate what the subject is and how you would like it to play out.

4) Fourth, sit in a very comfortable space and think. Breathe deeply down to your diaphragm and then stipulate through thought what your feeling and how you would like your outcome to be (if need be, read what you have written). Make sure that you go over this several times in order to get it in your mind. Don't be afraid of yourself. Depending on your *Level of Intent* is the *Level of your Outcome.* Try it. You can do no wrong as long as you have good intentions through your integrity.

Now, just like at the beginning of this chapter you can see how intent can effect a positive change in your life! Give it a try you will be surprised at how well we all work with each other through our consciousness.

Focusing Intent on a Particular Subject

Focusing intent on a particular subject takes timing and precision. Let's take timing for instance. Wouldn't you agree that all things happen for a reason and that timing matches those reasons?

Everything around us happens for a very specific reason and this specific reason is generated by timing and with precision. Your focus should go through many vibration layers and *precision* is focused exactness. Now all of this means really nothing to you, but to the spiritual consciousness this is the very product which our soul's live by. It is however, important that you understand this concept before attenuating a particular subject with a focus of intent.

Let us take an example:

Let's say, you own a business and you need funding through the government so you decide to send of a business plan that you created without direction from anything except your own knowledge gained through experience- However, the team that reviews these plans recognizes that you have left out some vital information. Now, it has taken you a number of months to create and develop this business plan and then several more months to learn that you are not qualified to earn government grants for your projects. Now, you fare rustrated (a negative feeling) and you are about to shut down because you can't bear any more of the cost.

In this example you would have tried to resolve a situation through the ego which no longer applies to the current circumstances, in short it doesn't work any longer.
What you should have done first was to have focused your newly found education to this set of circumstances through intent. It is one thing to really need help, but another when you know it and choose not to use this type of assistance.

So you focus your intent on this subject before you ever send it out. You apply the four levels of intent to your project and then you outline the outcome by stipulating what you really need. Then you sit down in a quiet place and recite it over and over again just as you reviewed your business plan over and over again to get it right. The only difference now, you will have applied the spiritual connection to the individual that will read your business plan and then the spiritual connection will lead that individual to talk to you about refining your plan to their needs instead of simply giving you a letter of rejection! You will have opened a door that will remain open all the way through your project.

It is really up to you to decide whether or not you wish to open this door or not. You can continued to slush through the mud the old fashion way or you can learn the new age way and fly through the air with the greatest of ease. You will have made a new business friend in the grant writing business that will support your interest each year as you request that funding that your company desperately needs.

It is also very important that you only focus with integrity and for the highest good to all, as well as no harm to all. If for any reason you choose not to follow this very important command you will suffer through negative karma instantly and it will manifest in a form different than the cause you once sought. By applying this frame of thought through a passive manner, then you open the doors to abundance for your sought after subject or cause.

Applying a Level of Intent in Variable Degrees

Now that you have your levels of intent down, you can start to look at other abilities that can be applied to intent. These variable degrees are energy vibrations which you apply to any given situation. For instance, say you want your child to do some chores around the house and you are asking him/or her for the first time. You would generally ask in a kind or friendly manner, right? Well, your energy vibration will come off as relaxed and happy. You are feeling good and satisfied that your child will follow through.

Now, say your child doesn't follow through and you become frustrated and angry so you request once again, but with greater intent and so your energy vibration is felt with an overpowering domination of the child. Now the child does the chore, but doesn't do a very good job at it and the energy vibrations you feel from your child are ill or frustrations. Now you both are frustrated. Why? Because you applied a negative energy vibration to a situation that you felt necessary to control. Now it is important to take some sort of control, however, it is important to take control in a positive manner rather than a negative one.

The positive approach to the situation is to give the child stewardship over the chore. In this manner the child learns through their mistakes as well as creates a sense of being able to accomplish a task. Positive reinforcement has a longer lasting effect than negative energy toward the child. Now, the child finished the job and you are now happy and the child is excited that he or she has earned the right to have their item back. The final outcome is positive for both you and the child.

Let us explore another situation:

Let;s say you are a manager in a well known company and you have to deal with a very difficult supervisor. This supervisor refuses to give you time off for a much needed surgery and your health lingers in the balance. You know it is only a matter of time before you wind up in the hospital unable to work, but your supervisor just doesn't care enough about you other than the work you can do to earn him or her a better bonus.

You are really upset over the ordeal so you try the traditional means of requesting the next four days off for the surgery. However, the supervisor says no and you will lose your job if you take the time off. You get even more upset. You try to explain in detail but he or she will have nothing to do regarding the details.   You realize that you don't have a voice in the matter of your own body, but the truth is you do!

See, you are trying to handle the situation by yourself in the ego principle so yes you are all alone. What a shame. Then you stop and think of how you can do better.

You remember that you read a book called "The Next Messiah –YOU"! You suddenly have an epiphany and you apply the "Levels of Intent" to your current situation. You figure that if this doesn't work, nothing will. Suddenly, your emotions shift and you feel empowered and you go through the levels and you place the energy vibrations out ahead of yourself and then you make the call to your supervisor. Ring! Ring! He or she picks up the phone,"Yah. What? You need the time off, why?" You tell that person why and they may or may not remember your request, but they give it to you without delay. There now you have your time off that is needed and you complete the task in a positive manner, you're happy and they are happy.

It isn't that hard to do. It really matters on the approach as to how the outcome will turn out. And it is all up to you! The more variable degrees of energy you apply to the situation the better the outcome will become. Remember to take back you power!!!

It is very important that you work with positive intentions verses negative intentions. The reason is simple. Do you prefer positive end results or would you prefer negative end results.

Since we are in a new age of consciousness, we no longer take centuries to suffer negative karma. This karmic energy is immediate and the rebuttal of energy in this particular time and space. Transversely it doesn't take century's to receive positive karma either. You will feel the results within minutes to days in this time and space.

You may or may not know that when operating on the this planet, at this particular time, you are operating as being human and you have accepted the consequences for your actions immediately so you will not carry negative karma into the next life path. This is a very good experience as you are perfecting in your own way to the father or deity that you believe in. If you don't believe in any deities or Father God then you must believe that you are the only one that supports yourself, so therefore why not experience all that you can while you live in this body!

Now I would like to reference how positive intent affects positive outcome. When working with energy you can control the vibration and the intensity as well as the energy itself. The energy itself has either positive or negative vibrations within it and you can control that by thought or thinking positive thoughts or negative thoughts at the time of the intention. The affects will mirror you intentions. If the intentions are of a positive nature then the outcome will always be positive in nature. If your intentions are negative in nature, then so will your outcome.

Oh, and by the way, this system isn't new, you have been using it since you were born into this life! Yes, it is true. However, you were not taught how it works and how to use it in a positive manner.

The ego principle doesn't teach you the vitality of life. It teaches you how to survive the ego principle life. The vitality of life is the very nature of your soul and of how you view spirit. This is why so many of you suffer cruelly, because you haven't been awakened into spiritual guidance, as of yet. You need to work at "Awakening."

It isn't easy bridging the gap from Ego Principle to God Consciousness. Think of it this way. You are only half the person that you could be if you remain in the ego principle for you entire life on this planet. Why would you only want to be half of your true potential? Most would agree it might look easier in short, but in the long run it isn't. You are always fighting to get through the mud with the ego, where in spirit you are always flying through time, space, and experiences, and it does, in fact, make it easier for you to experience the ego principle because now you will have learned how to work with it on a spiritual level.

In closing, here is some additional food for thought. Working with positive intent in spirit gives you the air to move through the physical energy of life (ego principle – illusion). This air is as abundant as you would like it to be and it will support the weight of any project on its back and send you flying through life in a very positive manner. However, if crossed you will suffer the negative karma that can ensue.

Remember to always keep your thoughts positive and keep educating yourself, for you are worth it in gold!

NOTES

CONCLUSION

The Next Messiah You, part one, is the beginning level of understanding spiritual guidance on a very basic level. But, completely different view and lessons through the still and God Consciousness. IT is the binary level of understanding in a world of so much incompleteness. The Next Messiah You trilogy set gives you the ability to recognize that you are not just a person working to survive but a person learning to live.

The Next Messiah You trilogy is about getting you off the beaten path like a pioneer on a wagon trail like you are now. Just as our wagon trial eased to wooden road ways and then onto paver stones and then eventually onto paved roads, so are you moving from the pioneering ways of religion into the spiritual ways of God Consciousness while enjoying the venture.

As The Next Messiah You, trilogy set adds to your paradigm form of thinking while building your knowledge to another paradigm and so on. These books are to help you move through the learning experiences with new knowledge and re-awakening into an era of self-realization without blindness.

We are creatures of habit and as long as we focus, we can achieve anything in any time and in any experience.

Come enjoy the expansion of mind, body, and soul through the teachings of God Consciousness.

Colophon

Titles: Walkway
Text: Minion Pro
formated in
Adobe Indesign 5.5
Printed in the USA

You may contact the author at

michaeldavid.author@gmail.com

www.onespiritpress.com
onespiritpress@gmail.com

www.ingramcontent.com/pod-product-compliance
Lightning Source LLC
Chambersburg PA
CBHW052010090426
42741CB00008B/1631